Human Rights

Other Books of Related Interest:

Opposing Viewpoints Series

China

North and South Korea

At Issue Series

Islamic Fundamentalism

United Nations

What Is the State of Human Rights?

"Congress shall make
no law . . . abridging
the freedom of speech,
or of the press."

First Amendment to the U.S. Constitution

The basic foundation of our democracy is the First Amendment guarantee of freedom of expression. The Opposing Viewpoints series is dedicated to the concept of this basic freedom and the idea that it is more important to practice it than to enshrine it.

OPPOSING VIEWPOINTS® SERIES

Human Rights

Jacqueline Langwith, Book Editor

GREENHAVEN PRESS

An imprint of Thomson Gale, a part of The Thomson Corporation

THOMSON
™
GALE

Detroit • New York • San Francisco • New Haven, Conn. • Waterville, Maine • London

THOMSON
GALE

Christine Nasso, *Publisher*
Elizabeth Des Chenes, *Managing Editor*

© 2008 The Gale Group.

Star logo is a trademark and Gale and Greenhaven Press are registered trademarks used herein under license.

For more information, contact:
Greenhaven Press
27500 Drake Rd.
Farmington Hills, MI 48331-3535
Or you can visit our Internet site at http://www.gale.com

LIBRARY OF CONGRESS CATALOGING-IN-PUBLICATION DATA

Human rights / Jacqueline Langwith, book editor.
    p. cm. -- Opposing Viewpoints
    Includes bibliographical references and index.
    ISBN-13: 978-0-7377-3745-5 (hardcover)
    ISBN-13: 978-0-7377-3746-2 (pbk.)
    1. Human rights. 2. Human rights--Government policy--United States. I. Langwith, Jacqueline.
    JC571.H866 2008
    323--dc22
                                                                                    2007029035

ISBN-10: 0-7377-3745-X
ISBN-10: 0-7377-3746-8

Printed in the United States of America
10 9 8 7 6 5 4 3 2 1

Contents

Why Consider Opposing Viewpoints?

> *"The only way in which a human being can make some approach to knowing the whole of a subject is by hearing what can be said about it by persons of every variety of opinion and studying all modes in which it can be looked at by every character of mind. No wise man ever acquired his wisdom in any mode but this."*
>
> *John Stuart Mill*

In our media-intensive culture it is not difficult to find differing opinions. Thousands of newspapers and magazines and dozens of radio and television talk shows resound with differing points of view. The difficulty lies in deciding which opinion to agree with and which "experts" seem the most credible. The more inundated we become with differing opinions and claims, the more essential it is to hone critical reading and thinking skills to evaluate these ideas. Opposing Viewpoints books address this problem directly by presenting stimulating debates that can be used to enhance and teach these skills. The varied opinions contained in each book examine many different aspects of a single issue. While examining these conveniently edited opposing views, readers can develop critical thinking skills such as the ability to compare and contrast authors' credibility, facts, argumentation styles, use of persuasive techniques, and other stylistic tools. In short, the Opposing Viewpoints series is an ideal way to attain the higher-level thinking and reading skills so essential in a culture of diverse and contradictory opinions.

In addition to providing a tool for critical thinking, Opposing Viewpoints books challenge readers to question their own strongly held opinions and assumptions. Most people form their opinions on the basis of upbringing, peer pressure, and personal, cultural, or professional bias. By reading carefully balanced opposing views, readers must directly confront new ideas as well as the opinions of those with whom they disagree. This is not to simplistically argue that everyone who reads opposing views will—or should—change his or her opinion. Instead, the series enhances readers' understanding of their own views by encouraging confrontation with opposing ideas. Careful examination of others' views can lead to the readers' understanding of the logical inconsistencies in their own opinions, perspective on why they hold an opinion, and the consideration of the possibility that their opinion requires further evaluation.

Evaluating Other Opinions

To ensure that this type of examination occurs, Opposing Viewpoints books present all types of opinions. Prominent spokespeople on different sides of each issue as well as well-known professionals from many disciplines challenge the reader. An additional goal of the series is to provide a forum for other, less-known, or even unpopular viewpoints. The opinion of an ordinary person who has had to make the decision to cut off life support from a terminally ill relative, for example, may be just as valuable and provide just as much insight as a medical ethicist's professional opinion. The editors have two additional purposes in including these less-known views. One, the editors encourage readers to respect others' opinions—even when not enhanced by professional credibility. It is only by reading or listening to and objectively evaluating others' ideas that one can determine whether they are worthy of consideration. Two, the inclusion of such viewpoints encourages the important critical thinking skill of objectively evaluating an author's credentials and bias. This evaluation will illuminate an author's reasons for taking a particular stance on an issue and will aid in readers' evaluation of the author's ideas.

It is our hope that these books will give readers a deeper understanding of the issues debated and an appreciation of the complexity of even seemingly simple issues when good and honest people disagree. This awareness is particularly important in a democratic society such as ours in which people enter into public debate to determine the common good. Those with whom one disagrees should not be regarded as enemies but rather as people whose views deserve careful examination and may shed light on one's own.

Thomas Jefferson once said that "difference of opinion leads to inquiry, and inquiry to truth." Jefferson, a broadly educated man, argued that "if a nation expects to be ignorant and free . . . it expects what never was and never will be." As individuals and as a nation, it is imperative that we consider the opinions of others and examine them with skill and discernment. The Opposing Viewpoints series is intended to help readers achieve this goal.

David L. Bender and Bruno Leone,
Founders

Introduction

"UNICEF's mission is to advocate for the protection of children's rights, to help meet their basic needs, and to expand their opportunities to reach their full potential. UNICEF is guided in doing this by the provisions and principles of the Convention on the Rights of the Child."

The United Nations
Children's Fund (UNICEF)

A round the world, millions of children suffer human rights abuses. Children in Nepal, Uganda, and the Congo are used as soldiers on the front lines of armed conflicts. Police in Bulgaria and Guatemala beat and torture homeless street children; disabled children in Romanian orphanages are confined to cribs for life, eating and defecating in their crib. Millions of children around the world, including in developed countries such as England and the United States, are subject to poverty, violence, rape, and cruelty.

The United Nations Convention on the Rights of the Child is meant to help end human rights violations against children. In some cases, governments may be responsible for perpetuating human rights violations against children. In other cases, governments may not be doing enough to protect children under their sovereignty. The United Nations Convention on the Rights of the Child (CRC) is the primary instrument available to help make governments responsible for protecting and ensuring children's rights.

The CRC is a component of international human rights law. The Universal Declaration of Human Rights provides the basic foundation of human rights law, declaring that all humans have certain inalienable rights. The CRC is one of six core treaties that build on the Universal Declaration to elaborate particular rights, set standards, and specify the rights of certain groups of people. In addition to the CRC, the six core treaties are the International Covenant on Civil and Political Rights (CCPR); the International Covenant on Economic, Social and Cultural Rights (CESCR); the Convention against Torture and Other Cruel, Inhuman or Degrading Treatment or Punishment (CAT); the International Convention on the Elimination of All Forms of Racial Discrimination (CERD); and the Convention on the Elimination of All Forms of Discrimination against Women (CEDAW). Many of the six core treaties are meant to protect especially vulnerable people such as children, women, minorities, and prisoners of war.

The CRC is organized around four guiding principles and provides fundamental rights, freedoms, and protections to people under the age of eighteen years old. Articles 2, 3, 6, and 12 embody the four main principles of the treaty: 1) The protection of children against discrimination; 2) Placing the best interests of the child before all other concerns; 3) Ensuring a child's right to life, survival, and development, and 4) Providing children the right to freedom of expression, particularly the ability to participate and voice their opinion in matters concerning themselves. Other protections offered by the CRC to children include the protection from violence, abuse, and abduction; the protection from hazardous employment and exploitation; the right to be free from military service (for those under the age of fifteen); and the right to education and adequate health care.

The CRC is used as a tool by many child-focused humanitarian organizations. According to the United Nations Children's Fund (UNICEF), the CRC has succeeded in protecting children in the following ways:

- In Rwanda, children were moved out of adult detention centers, where they had been held for alleged war offenses, and transferred to special juvenile institutions where they were assigned lawyers to defend them.

- In Belgium and Germany, laws inspired by the Convention extended the ability of national authorities to prosecute cases of child prostitution and pornography.

- In Romania, CRC principles helped change adoption laws, guide training for magistrates to address juvenile delinquency, and reform the child protection system.

- In Vietnam, UNICEF used the CRC to help the Ministry of Justice and nongovernmental organizations to implement an appropriate judicial process for juveniles, as well as to train judges, police, and other legal professionals on child-friendly policies in line with the Convention.

- After ratifying the CRC, El Salvador, Peru, and Bolivia all enacted new justice codes for children.

Despite these apparent successes not everyone is happy with the CRC or its use by humanitarian organizations. The CRC was adopted by the United Nations in 1989 and since then has been ratified by all but two countries, Somalia and the United States. The United States has not ratified the CRC primarily because of concerns that it interferes with parental rights and family life. The conservative think tank, the Heritage Foundation, lists many CRC-based directives issued by the United Nations Committee on the Rights of the Child that it believes undermine family, religion, and United States sovereignty. For instance, the Heritage Foundation takes issue with a recommendation to Belize that the country set up legal mechanisms to help children challenge their parents' violation of their rights and a recommendation to Russia that the country ensure access for adolescents to sex education including information about contraception.

Some groups believe that UNICEF focuses too much attention on the CRC and not enough on child survival. In 2005, Peter Horton, editor of the prestigious British medical journal, *The Lancet*, urged UNICEF to shift away from its CRC-based approach and to return to the organization's original focus on "raw child survival." Horton said the "language of rights means little to a child stillborn, an infant dying in pain from pneumonia, or a child desiccated by famine." Horton and others believe that UNICEF's focus on rights has been to the detriment of children, millions of whom are dying from preventable illnesses before they reach the age of five.

Recognizing children's vulnerability, the CRC treaty provides a distinctive set of safeguards to protect them from harm and promote their upbringing in a safe and happy environment. Amnesty International says, "As human beings, children are entitled to all the rights guaranteed by the Universal Declaration of Human Rights, but children also need special protection and care." The treaty has fostered gains in children's rights, but some people believe that implementation of the CRC threatens traditional family values, while others believe that UNICEF's focus on the CRC has weakened the organization and threatens child survival.

Debates about human rights are particularly poignant because they generally occur against a backdrop of human suffering. Those who study and write about human rights are often seeking answers to difficult questions, such as what is the best way to prevent children from being used in armed conflicts, or how can the lives of children in orphanages be made better. In *Opposing Viewpoints: Human Rights* the contributors discuss human rights issues in the following chapters: What Are Human Rights? What Is the State of Human Rights? What Should Be Done to Stop Human Rights Abuses? And What Human Rights Policies Should the U.S. Government Follow?

What Are Human Rights?

Chapter Preface

According to the organization NetAid, over a billion people live in extreme poverty, defined as living on less than one U.S. dollar a day. Additionally, each year over 8 million people die because they are simply too poor to stay alive and more than 800 million people go hungry every day. According to the organization Freedom House, 2,448,600,000 people across the world, roughly 37 percent of the global population, live in repressive countries deemed by the organization as being "not free." These statements reflect two different human rights concerns and comprise support for each side on what is sometimes called the "food versus freedom" debate. Some people think that economic and social rights are more important, while others believe that civil and political rights are more important.

Since it began in the 1960s, the modern human rights movement has typically focused on first-generation human rights. First-generation human rights are civil and political in nature and serve to protect the individual from excesses of government. First-generation rights include freedom of speech, the right to a fair trial, freedom of religion, and voting rights. It was outrage over the trampling of these first-generation rights that led to the formation of the world's first modern human rights organization, Amnesty International. The organization was started in 1961 by a group of Englishmen outraged over the sentencing of two Portuguese college students to twenty years in prison for having raised their glasses in a toast to "freedom" in a bar. Over the years Amnesty International and other human rights groups have worked to bring attention to repressive governments, to free people unjustly imprisoned, and to abolish torture and the death penalty.

Economic, social, and cultural (ESC) rights are second-generation rights. These rights relate to the conditions necessary to meet basic human needs such as food, shelter, education, health care, and gainful employment. They include the rights to education, adequate housing, food, water, the highest attainable standard of health, the right to work and rights at work, the right to a healthy environment, and the cultural rights of minorities and indigenous peoples.

Some people have questioned the wisdom of the human rights movement's (particularly Amnesty International's) focus on ESC rights, saying it dilutes their effectiveness in fighting for civil and political rights. In March 2007, the editors of the conservative magazine, the *Economist*, asserted that ESC rights are distractions to civil and political human rights. They said, "Rights being good things, you might suppose that the more of them you campaign for the better. Why not add pressing social and economic concerns to stuffy old political rights such as free speech, free elections and due process of law? What use is a vote if you are starving? Are not access to jobs, housing, health care, and food basic rights too? No: few rights are truly universal, and letting them multiply weakens them." The editors of the *Economist* and others, believe it is more important to protect civil and political rights than ESC rights.

However, others disagree. Some people believe that the right to adequate food, housing, education, and health care is paramount. They think that people need to be free from poverty before they can ever be free from the excesses of government. Columbia University professor Thomas Pogge, has said, "Piecing together the global record, we find that most of the current massive underfulfillment of human rights is more or less directly connected to poverty. Desperately poor people, often stunted, illiterate, and heavily preoccupied with the struggle to survive, typically lack effective means for resisting or rewarding their rulers, who are therefore likely to rule them oppressively."

Still other people think that drawing distinctions between human rights are a disservice to humankind. In response to the *Economist* editorial, Vincent Villano replied, "by recognizing the interdependence of civil, political, economic, social and cultural rights we can better assess the state of human rights in our world and acquire a sense of where and how we must begin the important mission of realizing them."

The debate about ESC rights versus civil and political rights also includes the concept of negative versus positive rights. Within the philosophy of human rights, some people make a distinction between positive rights and negative rights. A positive right imposes a moral obligation on a person or the government *to do something* for an individual, while a negative right, obliges the government *not to do something*, i.e. intervene in an individual's life. ESC rights, like ensuring food, housing, and health care are seen as positive rights. On the other hand, civil and political rights are associated with negative rights because they oblige the government not to interfere with individual freedoms. Some people, such as the editors of the *Economist*, say that only negative rights are truly universal and that ensuring positive rights like adequate housing, food, and water invites the government to intervene in people's lives and runs the risk of giving the government too much control.

The debate about ESC rights versus civil and political rights suggests that in spite of the Universal Declaration of Human Rights and the core human rights treaties, there is no consensus on which rights are truly universal human rights. The contributors in the following chapter also illustrate this point as they provide more viewpoints and discussion about the meaning and origin of the concept of human rights.

> "If human rights are portrayed as culturally relative then they can be denied to certain groups."

Human Rights Must Be Universal

Fiona Boylan, Integrated Regional Information Networks

In this viewpoint, Integrated Regional Information Networks (IRIN), part of the United Nations Office for the Coordination of Humanitarian Affairs, stresses the importance of the universality of human rights. IRIN affirms that human rights are seen purely as a construct of the United States, France, and other countries in the West. Restricting human rights to Westerners gives non-Western countries an "out" for violating human rights treaties, and it justifies human rights abuses in non-Western locations. The IRIN emphasizes that human rights must be viewed as universal; otherwise, they will be denied to some groups of people. The IRIN provides news and analysis about sub-Saharan Africa, the Middle East, and Central Asia for the humanitarian community.

As you read, consider the following questions:

1. According to the Integrated Regional Information Networks (IRIN), what idea about human rights did Presidents Marcos and Suharto and Prime Minister Yew advocate?

2. Saudi Arabia's agreement to adopt the Universal Declaration of Human Rights in 1948 only to the extent that it did not violate Shari'a Law demonstrated what, according to the IRIN?

3. Who does the IRIN quote as saying, "Freedom from torture and genocide, freedom from hunger and persecution, freedom to worship and to express opinions, the right to fairness at trial, and so on, are not western inventions—they are your entitlement as a human being whether you live in London or Nairobi, Timbuktu or Tuvalu?"

The development of human rights is often charted by reference to the Magna Carta (1215), the American Bill of Rights (ratified in 1791) and the French Revolution (1789). These are considered landmark events that culminated in the Universal Declaration of Human Rights.

The Magna Carta granted certain rights to noble landowners in England, but did little to enfranchise the common man. The American Bill of Rights, and the constitution established following the French Revolution, codified the rights of the citizens of those nations, "as individuals". They were the political manifestations of philosophical advances going on during the age of Enlightenment. The developments focused on the rights of the individual as distinguishable from the society and the state—rights which had not existed before. A new age dawned in which "natural, inalienable and sacred rights" were recognised as belonging to citizens, giving them the power and the standing to challenge those who governed them oppressively.

These benefits were extended to all citizens of the countries that signed the 1948 Universal Declaration of Human Rights. The declaration stated that "recognition of the inherent dignity and/or the equal and inalienable rights of all members of the human family is the foundation of freedom, justice and peace in the world."

Cultural Imperialism and Cultural Relativism

The danger is that if authorship is attributed as a progression from western philosophy to the Universal Declaration, then the drive for human rights can be viewed as a western ideal; therefore, the imposition of such rights on non-western nations is a form of cultural imperialism.

This leads to the argument for cultural relativism, an argument which suggests that human rights are not a universal concept but are, in effect, regional depending on the norms of each society.

The Bogus Asian Values Debate

In the late 1990s, the former prime minister of Singapore, Lee Kuan Yew, following Presidents [Ferdinand] Marcos and Suharto, both of Indonesia, advocated the idea that individual human rights are antithetical to Asian and African mores; he argued that these rights need not be extended to the peoples of those areas. All three presidents believed that the concept of universal human rights should not be applied to societies that emphasise the greater good of society as a whole—a form of collective human rights—above those of the individual.

The debate, which Justice Geoffrey Robertson, Queens Council jurist and author has referred to as the "bogus Asian values debate", has been coloured by the many human rights abuses recorded under the regimes of those proponents. The disdain shown for the rights of individuals or minorities was encapsulated in a statement which Lee Kuan Yew made when addressing business leaders at a dinner in 1999. Referring to the well-documented human rights abuses occurring In Timor-Leste he said: "There are many unhappy minorities living very uncomfortable lives in ASEAN (Association of Southeast Asian Nations). You know that, I know that. We look the other way. To go in and intervene would have the whole ASEAN solidarity breaking up."

The issue is that acknowledging the rights of the individual, or even minorities, can upset the equilibrium and be to the detriment of society as a whole; in this case 'society' refers to the ASEAN bloc. Put another way, the greater good is not served by according rights to individuals. . . .

Revolutionary and Recent Rights

The question remains, though, if the development of human rights is understood to stem from western philosophy, whether this is relevant to the debate on the applicability of human rights to all. In other words, does the provenance of human rights dictate the applicability?

Dr An-Na'Im, Charles Howard Candler Professor of Law at Emory University, Atlanta, rejects the basis of the discussion on the grounds that the development of human rights is not exclusively western. He believes that is "an oversimplification of an enlightened, pluralistic west, versus a despotic and authoritarian east". He sees "the human rights paradigm" as "the child of the UN Universal Declaration on Human Rights" established in 1948, and as such as "revolutionary and recent".

An-Na'Im argues that the American Bill of Rights and the French Constitution "were concerned with the citizens of those countries, not with the rights to be accorded to all human beings", and that it was this classification that allowed the European Enlightenment to legitimise colonisation, which valued the life of the citizens above those of other human beings. He believes this was responsible for countless human rights

abuses, and displayed considerable cynicism and hypocrisy:
the basic rights to life and self-determination were denied to
many, while the Europeans congratulated themselves on their
internal, national development of social ideas, individual rights
and philanthropic enterprises.

Shari'a Law and Human Rights

On the question of whether human rights can coexist with
Shari'a law [traditional Islamic law] An-Na'Im asserts that
"human rights are the means by which people come to assert
their own voice, their own interpretation of religion and culture, and thereby affirm the universality of all human rights,
including the right to understand Shari'a as supportive, and
not hostile to, human rights". He does allow that much of
Shari'a law, as currently interpreted, can be hostile to fundamental human rights, most particularly those of women.

This basic opposition between Shari'a law and human rights was most clearly demonstrated by Saudi Arabia's agreement to adopt the Universal Declaration on Human Rights in 1948 only to the extent that it did not conflict with Shari'a law. However, he draws a distinction: "It was the ruling regime of Saudi Arabia, monarchy, which took that position, and not the people of Arabia by their own free choice. . . . A certain elite made that decision in the name of people who continue to be victims of human rights violations. That position is also taken in the name of religion and culture, but it is self-appointed guardians of religion and culture who claim that voice, to the exclusion of other voices among believers and within the culture."

He states that "Theologically, Islam is a radically democratic religion because every Muslim has the religious obligation to determine for herself or himself what is the position of Shari'a on every issue," and that there is a growing body of Muslims who do not view Shari'a and human rights as incompatible. The modernisation of society has allowed people to have greater access to education and to assess the words of the Sunna—the words, sayings and deeds of the Prophet Mohammed and the Qur'an. He argues that this means that the "theology and sociology of Islam are coming together to liberate Muslims from archaic views of Shari'a. Human rights are part of the means and ends of this transformation."

The Qur'an is obviously immutable, but a more modern Ijtihad, or application of human reason in the interpretation of Shari'a, a reading which emphasises the rights and obligations of the individual, could, in his opinion, reconcile perceived differences. He goes so far as to say: "Islamic societies are now going through a type of Reformation. When Christian societies were going through this they were not necessarily aware of it at the time. The magnitude of change is often understood in retrospect." This alleged Reformation can seem a long way off in a time when mere cartoons of the Prophet

Mohmammed can cause riots and bloodshed across the world, and when fatwas are issued against those perceived to be at odds with the message of Islam.

In his essay, "Is Personal Freedom a Western Value?", Thomas Franck—writing in the *American Journal of International Law* in 1997—points out: "In the Human Rights Committee, a UN body which has now been replaced by the Human Rights Council, Islamic members have been among the most outspoken in rejecting the notion of incompatibility between Islamic law and the global law of the human rights treaty system". This suggests that the idea that Islamic law and human rights are fundamentally incompatible is a view held by only a few Islamic countries.

Nevertheless, this is not often discussed in the western media. Instead of analysing the development of human rights from a non-western perspective, there is a perception that before the Universal Declaration the concept of human rights did not exist in such countries. The focus tends to be on the differences in cultures and what some have termed the more 'barbaric' aspects of Shari'a law.

When discussing the human rights framework and its universal applicability, debate often dwells on the repression of women in many Arabic societies, and the extreme forms of punishment, such as cutting off the hands of thieves. It is often forgotten that these practices, including stoning people to death, are only advocated by the more extreme factions within the Islamic religion and that the Qur'an does not prescribe such activities.

"Tribal" Differences

That is not to deny that these practices do go on, and frequently. Signing-up to conventions is laudable, but it is only paying lip service to the idea of inalienable human rights, if those rights are not respected. When outrage is not felt across the Muslim world when a woman is stoned to death for adultery, some observers in the west claim this [is] a proof that human rights are denied in these countries and this is a result of cultural incompatibility between human rights and Islamic law.

The fact that reports emerge from certain Islamic countries of women being stoned for adultery and that echoes of outrage do not seem to ripple across the Islamic world leads some observers to believe that basic human rights are routinely denied as a result of the cultural incomparability of human rights treaties and Islamic law.

However, there is a difference between advocating against the infringement of human rights in certain parts of the world and presenting human rights as fundamentally foreign to those parts of the world. As Justice Geoffrey Robertson Q.C. points out: "Freedom from torture and genocide, freedom from hunger and persecution, freedom to worship and to express opinions, the right to fairness at trial, and so on, are not western inventions—they are your entitlement as a human being, whether you live in London or Nairobi, Timbuktu or Tuvalu. On this issue there can be no compromise, no excuse of 'cultural relativism.'"

"There are some backsliders in the human rights movement who think that evils like female genital mutilation can be excused as 'culturally relative' because they have happened to a lot of women in Africa, for a long time. That does not justify the practice: it is a form of torture, for which there can be no justification. . . . Tribal or national practices that are, objectively, barbaric and primitive, cannot be countenanced."

To those who reject the universality and inalienability of human rights, this attitude smacks of cultural imperialism.

Toward Universality

The concept of human rights has, since 1948 and the Universal Declaration, entered the mainstream. The language of human rights has long been used in the realms of politics and diplomacy, and it is not unusual for political pressure to be brought to bear on countries in order for them to improve their human rights record. Just one example is the efforts that Turkey has been required to make in order for discussions to begin on its possible accession to the European Union.

However, this language has only recently been given force at a legal level. There have been dramatic steps forward in the international arena in the last fifteen years [1992 to 2007] towards making people accountable for the human rights abuses they have committed. This is a remarkable step forward from dialogue to enforcement. The International Criminal Tribunals for the former Yugoslavia and for Rwanda, as well as the setting up of the International Criminal Court, are evidence of commitments to combat the systematic infringement of human rights at an international, legal level.

At last, there is the prospect of power behind the word and concepts.

There is little doubt that despite the grand words in treaties and conventions, the drive to accord all humans with basic rights is a theory not yet practised. There are widespread abuses, sometimes governmental, sometimes stemming from war, and sometimes as part of centuries-old practices that communities are loathe to relinquish. It is this last category that proves the thorniest issue in terms of cultural relativism and potential allegations of imperialism.

Yet, unless the human rights themselves are seen as universally relevant to all humans, such attempts will be open to the accusation that they are a form of cultural imperialism or even an irrelevance to certain peoples. If human rights are portrayed as culturally relative then they can be denied to certain groups. If the language of human rights is allowed to be politicised, 'relativised' or hijacked for other reasons, this fuels distrust for the aims of human rights treaties or organizations and alienates peoples from a supposedly Universal Declaration on Human Rights.

"Human rights, while universal in their application, can't be universal in their acceptance because of who we are, where we come from and what we believe."

Human Rights Must Be Culturally Relative

Jieh-Yung Lo

In this viewpoint, Jieh-Yung Lo challenges the notion that human rights should have one "universal" definition that is accepted by people of all cultures throughout the world. Lo says Asian cultures and values in particular pose a challenge to the universality of human rights because generally Asian values are different than the values of Western society. For instance, western cultures place greater emphasis on the rights of individuals whereas Asian cultures tend to value the rights of communities over the rights of individuals. Jieh-Yung Lo is the policy officer for the Ethnic Communities Council of Victoria, Australia, an advocacy group representing ethnic minorities.

Jieh-Yung Lo, "Universalism Challenged—Human Rights and Asian Values," *On Line Opinion*, February 1, 2007. Reproduced by permission.

As you read, consider the following questions:

1. According to Jieh-Yung Lo, the emergence of what two countries has sparked the debate about common sets of values?

2. The Asian values' challenge to the universality of human rights can be seen in what three terms, according to this author? Explain.

3. How does this author say Asians view the continuation of Lee Kuan Yew's prime ministership of Singapore?

I was raised in a very traditional Chinese family in Australia. My values and ethics are a convergence of two different cultures. As I get older I realise that human rights, while universal in their application, can't be universal in their acceptance because of who we are, where we come from and what we believe. This is not necessarily a problem, but we must understand that our ethics and values are not homogenous and it is culture that poses the challenge to the universality of human rights.

Asian Values

The universality of human rights today has come into conflict with some of the oldest traditions in human history. The emergence of China and India, both economically and socially, has meant western culture has had to engage with a different ethical structure that I call "Asian values". This development has sparked some debate about common sets of values and who has the right to impose values upon others.

Clearly, a general view of an Asian value system would argue that its ideals are not drawn from the more individualistic notion of human rights that is common within western culture.

In reality, our ideals and values are diverse as ever. This makes for a healthy democracy. But how then do we develop policy to reflect diversity? Even human rights, which we assume in the West are universal, may be different depending on one's culture, religion or family. Asian values have influenced and governed the lives of Asian cultures for centuries and as history has shown, its success is in its survival.

Asian Cultures Promote Other Values

Rather than focusing on individualism and democracy, Asian values provide greater emphasis on the moral and collective duties of a human being. The notion of rights is based more around "duties" to other human beings. These can be to parents, friends, traditions and the greater interest of the community, which are the main concerns in most Asian cultures and societies.

To sum it up, the community takes precedence over individuals, social and economic rights take precedence over civil and political rights, and rights themselves are a matter of national sovereignty.

For example, my parents' instilling the importance of a good education is not about my individual achievement, but about representing my family and focusing on what my achievements bring to others. A good education leads to gaining a promising job, which in turn brings prestige and honour to the family and the capacity to support them into the future. Family forms the core value of my responsibilities.

My decision to continue to live with my parents and to assist in taking responsibility of paying bills shows a strong sign of the duties emphasised in Asian cultures. Rather than fight the idea that the money I earn is mine, I accept that my role is to contribute to the family and community in which I live. These obligations and commitments to duties don't fit within a generally accepted human rights framework, as I understand it.

All People Do Not Aspire to the Same Rights

The 1948 Universal Declaration of Human Rights may be formally accepted around the world, but its generalized framework allows for almost limitless interpretations. Even the supposed global consensus on, say, the prohibition of torture as a "human wrong" is deceptive: In the aftermath of the terror attacks of September 11, 2001, the prominent U.S. legal scholar Alan Dershowitz argued in favor of legalized torture as a counterterror measure.

If anything, the postcolonial period since the writing of the declaration has witnessed an erosion of the belief in the universality of human aspirations. In part, this erosion stems from a widespread conviction that human rights are a Western invention being shoved down non-Western throats. Though such attitudes are partly a propaganda ploy by leaders who seek to shield their abusive behavior from criticism, they also reflect the views of many non-Westerners who believe that the highly individualistic declaration does not adequately balance rights with responsibilities—witness the emergence of "Asian Values" or "Islamic Values."

Richard Falk, *"Human Rights. (Think Again),"*
Foreign Policy, *March–April 2004, pp. 18–24.*

Asian Values Challenge Human Rights Universality

The Asian values challenge to the universality of human rights can be seen in three terms: cultural, economic, and political. Culturally, they assert that the Western approach ignores the specific cultural traditions and historical circumstances of Asian societies.

Economically, they maintain that the priority of developing Asian societies is to eradicate poverty and the right to survival must come first.

And politically, having political stability under a capable leadership of good governance is essential to the survival of a nation and its culture.

This doesn't mean that Asian values support dictatorships; it just means people who are bounded by these values tend to work for the continuation of its culture and the growth of the nation, rather than for individual gains.

For example, the continuation of Lee Kuan Yew's prime ministership is seen as a breach of democratic values, but in terms of Asian culture the continuation of his leadership ensures substantial and uninterrupted growth for Singapore. The criticisms of Asian societies' human rights record has shown that observers fail to acknowledge other elements and values that Asian cultures promote.

Cultural Relativism

There has been a controversial belief that the concept of human rights is, by and large, a Western cultural norm, which is often at odds with non-Western cultures and, therefore, not applicable in non-Western societies. The Universal Declaration of Human Rights reflects this deep-rooted and popular assumption. It is culture, not the political, religious or ethnic that is providing the main obstacle to achieving a universal system of human rights. We should not all pursue human rights in the same way.

It is vital that observers acknowledge the cultural diversity and relativism that exist among societies. A call for cross-cultural dialogue and cross-national engagements on the universality of human rights is needed. Western societies should acknowledge the fact that other cultures have their own beliefs and systems of living.

> "The debate between the 2 classic positions [universalism and cultural relativism] is not a relevant or useful dichotomy."

We Should Eliminate the Debate About Universality and Cultural Relativism

El Obaid Ahmed El Obaid

El Obaid Ahmed El Obaid contends that the argument between those that believe human rights are "universal" and those that believe they are "culturally relative" is irrelevant and useless, and he says both positions are flawed. According to El Obaid, the events since September 11, 2001, have shown that universalism has failed. Moreover, cultural relativism has never had a credible claim. El Obaid believes that true progress will come about when we focus our attentions on enforcing the rights and freedoms that we all agree upon. El Obaid Ahmed El Obaid is the chief counselor for the Ministry of Human Rights of Yemen/United Nations Development Program.

El Obaid Ahmed El Obaid, "Universalism and Cultural Relativism," *International Center for Human Rights Education*, June 18, 2004, www.equitas.org/english/programs/downloads/ihrtp-proceedings/25th/Eng_Universalism-and-Cultural-R.pdf. Reproduced by permission.

As you read, consider the following questions:

1. What does El Obaid believe are some of the traditional definitions of culture?

2. What does El Obaid say is at the center of the universal conception of human rights?

3. What does El Obaid claim about most of the people who raise the notion of cultural relativism?

The notion of cultural relativism or cultural diversity came out of the discussion related to the origins of human rights. Some of the traditional texts claim that human rights originated in Europe and came out of western documents. Therefore there is an element of contention whenever we talk about the origins of human rights.

What Is Culture?

It is extremely difficult to define culture. Culture is an elusive term—it can mean almost anything. Some of the traditional definitions of culture state that culture represents a number of norms that influence our perception of the whole world. No matter how we define culture, it deeply affects human behaviour.

Human rights violations relate to human acts or omissions. Acts are positive steps to harm someone or deny them physical or mental well-being. Omissions occur when people are indifferent towards the suffering and violation of others' rights.

We cannot exclude culture—there is no human rights discourse or practice that exists in a cultural vacuum. Human rights practice is always contextual—we are always dealing with cultural practices that assist or impede our human rights work. It is therefore important to talk about culture when we talk about human rights.

The Two Classic Positions

1. Human rights are universal.

This conception of rights places the protection of the independent individual at the centre, and the individual is assumed to be a self-sufficient entity. It follows that this is the only possible conception of human rights. This set of rights has been determined—either you accept these rights or not. Rights therefore bring with them a degree of finality and imposition.

2. Human rights are culturally relative.

This position advocates that each and every culture has its own notion of human rights and freedoms. Human rights can only exist by reverting back to cultural norms, not looking to external (Western, legal) documents. Each group should look to their own culture to devise and implement their own notion of rights. Employing the universalist concept of rights or using the available international instruments is a form of cultural imperialism.

These are representations of extreme universalist and cultural relativist positions. Each position tries to make its case by indicting the other position. For a universalist, talking about culture endangers human rights by allowing cultures that have harmful practices to dilute the notion of rights. For a relativist, allowing the notion of universalism is accepting alien values and Western imperialism.

Relativism Versus Universalism

The debate between the 2 classic positions is not a relevant or useful dichotomy for several reasons:

- The dichotomy is circular. There is no way to make a convincing argument that certain conceptions originated in one culture and not in another. It is simply untrue that any one culture has remained intact and without outside influence throughout history.

The Human Rights Debate

Typically the scholarly debate over human rights is thought to take place between two opposing camps: the universalists and the cultural relativists. The universalists build their understanding of human rights upon the liberal tradition whereby rights are accorded to the individual by virtue of being human. Cultural relativists, on the other hand, argue that values are grounded in specific communities and that the communal group, not the individual, is the basic social unit. In reality, however, the ideological spectrum is much more complex; realizing that complexity can help point us to where the challenges to international human rights actually lie.

Joanne Bauer,
Carnegie Council for Ethics in International Affairs,
March 26, 2003. www.cceia.org.

- The concept of universalism has failed. After the September 11th [2001] bombings we realized that there is no model for an ideal version of human rights. The practices of the states who are aggressive in advancing the notion of universalism changed in the aftermath of the bombings. It has now been deemed acceptable for these states to conduct racial profiling and to exclude certain groups from the protection of human rights on the basis that they are different.

- There is no credible claim for upholding cultural relativism. Most of the people who raise the notion of cultural relativism are human rights violators themselves, whether they are in government like a number of Middle Eastern and Asian states, or whether they are in other spheres like the NGO [nongovernmental organizations] sector. When relativists use the word culture they are invoking an idealistic, rigid, static notion of culture. Cultural relativism is used as a guise for political or economic gain, and not as a commitment to the higher values and ideals of the protection of human rights.

A Different Approach

For a change we should start looking at areas in which there are no differences. We need to draw up a list of the rights and freedoms that are not contentious and that do not present difficulties. It would be surprising to many of us to discover that the rights we agree upon represent 80–90% of all human rights. We need to ask what we are doing to reinforce those rights and freedoms that are not controversial. This approach is much more positive and constructive. The true progress would be the enforcement of those rights and this is what we have to work towards.

> "The belief that the current international human rights regime is derived exclusively from the ideological framework of the West is a major obstacle in its acceptance as a truly universal vision."

Non-Western Societies Have Influenced Human Rights

Faisal Kutty

In the following viewpoint, Faisal Kutty disputes the notion that the concept of human rights was developed in the West. Kutty says non-Western societies have valid conceptions of human rights, although they are different than those contained in the Universal Declaration. Asian and Islamic cultures value individual rights along with collective rights, or the rights of the community. Kutty believes that the United Nations should reformulate the Universal Declaration of Human Rights so that it is more inclusive of non-Western conceptions and is truly "universal." Faisal Kutty is a lawyer and writer in Canada.

Faisal Kutty, "A Western Construct? The Legacy of the Universal Declaration of Human Rights," *www.counterpunch.org*, December 9, 2006. Reproduced by permission.

As you read, consider the following questions:

1. According to Kutty, former First Lady Eleanor Roosevelt drew comparisons between the Universal Declaration of Human Rights and what other international document?

2. How many countries voted for the Universal Declaration of Human Rights, according to the author? Which countries abstained and expressed reservations?

3. According to Kutty, who said "I think a universal concept of human rights must come from the philosophical vision of all peoples?"

Fifty-eight years after the universal declaration of human rights was adopted by the United Nations General Assembly, the debate continues as to whether the document is truly universal.

Upon its adoption on Dec. 10, 1948, former U.S. First Lady Eleanor Roosevelt, chair of the commission on human rights, expressed her hope it would become "the Magna Carta of all mankind." Ironically, as was the fate with the "great charter" of 1215, the declaration has not fully lived up to its name.

Conflicting Views on Universal Declaration

The declaration was challenged from its very inception. The commission's first draft attracted 168 amendments from various countries. However, the final document was almost unchanged from the initial draft tabled by the commission. Forty-eight countries voted in favour, while eight countries—Poland, Byelorussia, Czechoslovakia, the Ukraine, Yugoslavia, South Africa, Saudi Arabia and the Soviet Union—abstained and expressed reservations.

The conflicting views on the declaration have become more pronounced recently as human rights take a more cen-

Magna Carta,
Origin of Human Rights?!

People in the West have the habit of attributing every beneficial development in the world to themselves. For example, it is vociferously claimed that the world first derived the concept of basic human rights from the *Magna Carta* of Britain—which was drawn up six hundred years after the advent of Islam. But the truth is that until the seventeenth century no one dreamt of arguing that the *Magna Carta* contained the principles of trial by jury, *Habeas Corpus* and control by Parliament of the right of taxation. If the people who drafted the *Magna Carta* were living today they would be greatly surprised to be told that their document enshrined these ideals and principles.

To the best of my knowledge, the West had no concept of human and civic rights before the seventeenth century; and it was not until the end of the eighteenth century that the concept took on practical meaning in the constitutions of America and France.

Jamaat-e-Islami Pakistan Islam:
Meaning and Message—The Political Framework of Islam,
http://jamaat.org/islam/HumanRightsPolitical.html.

tral role in international and domestic forums. The critics of the current international human rights standards range from cultural relativists and Islamists to proponents of Asian values. They contend the existing international human rights regime is deeply influenced by the western experience. The spotlight on the individual, the focus on rights divorced from duties, the emphasis on legalism to secure these rights and the greater priority given to civil and political rights are all hallmarks of the western bias. In contrast, the Asian (including Buddhist, Taoist, Confucian, Hindu, etc.) and Islamic conceptions would emphasize community, duties to one another and society, and some even place greater emphasis on economic, social and cultural rights.

Individualism at Odds with Non-Western Ideologies

The philosophical and ideological underpinnings defining human relationship with each other and society in many non-Western societies are at variance with our fixation with individualism or what some would call radical individualism.

The focus on individual rights—in some cases to the detriment of the family and community—is not consistent with many non-Western outlooks on human rights.

Confucian scholar Tu Weiming writes: "Confucian humanism offers an account of the reasons for supporting basic human rights that does not depend on a liberal conception of persons."

Individualism and Collectivism Can Coexist

However, this in no way implies that such views are totally devoid of consideration for the individual. The substructures of human rights in some non-Western conceptions attempt to establish equilibrium between individualism and collectivism in ways that are different from ours. Far from being a contradiction, as documented by collectivists theorists such as Harry Triandis, individualism and collectivism can coexist and in fact can thrive together.

From the Confucian perspective, for instance, Weiming notes: "Human rights are inseparable from human responsibilities."

Although in the Confucian tradition, duty-consciousness is more pronounced than rights-consciousness—to the extent that the Confucian tradition underscores self-cultivation, family cohesiveness, economic well-being, social order, political justice and cultural flourishing—it is a valuable spring of wisdom for an understanding of human rights broadly conceived.

The natural law origin of the declaration also conflicts with the religious view that rights are derived from divine authority. Brazil's suggestion [that] the declaration ought to have referred to a transcendent entity was rejected outright during the debate leading to the declaration's adoption. One argument says the denial of divine authority is essential to make the philosophy underlying rights protection universal. How can something be universal when it rejects the view of a significant component of the world's population—not only eastern religions but also adherents of Christianity and Judaism—who believe in some form of divine authority? Why should the assumption of secular elite be imposed on everyone?

The extensive list of fundamental human rights is subject to certain general limitations, set out in articles 29 and 30 of the declaration. Article 29 (2), for instance, provides for "limitations as are determined by law solely for the purpose of securing due recognition and respect for the rights and freedoms of others and of meeting the just requirements of morality, public order and the general welfare in a democratic society." The different philosophies and views undoubtedly will produce equally valid interpretations of such restrictive articles and human rights standards in general.

Freedom Is Not Just a Western Construct

A strong argument can be made that the current formulation of international human rights constitutes a cultural structure in which western society finds itself easily at home. This has led some western human-rights scholars to arrogantly conclude that most non-western societies lack not only the practice of human rights but also the very concept. This clearly overlooks the fact that we can only claim to be better than others because we use our own values and standards to measure them.

Dominance cannot be equated with the truth, though it is easy to get caught up in the old confusion between might and right.

It is important to acknowledge and appreciate that other societies may have equally valid alternative conceptions of human rights. Exiled Tunisian Islamist leader Rachid Ghannouchi once told a reporter: "I think a universal concept of human rights must come from the philosophical vision of all peoples."

The call for a more inclusive conception is laudable, particularly given that even proponents of the other views acknowledge that there are certain universal values. For instance, the jailed former deputy prime minister of Malaysia, Anwar Ibrahim, a proponent of both Asian values and Islam, writes in his book, *The Asian Renaissance*, "To say that freedom is western . . . is to offend our own traditions as well as our forefathers, who gave their lives in the struggle against tyranny and injustice."

Claims of universality do not ensure universal acceptance. Accommodating the various conceptions within the international framework may or may not be plausible. The difficulty of the task should not prevent us from grappling with this issue. At least from this exercise we may in fact learn that there are indeed certain truly universal ideals and principles shared by us all.

Belief in Western Origin Is a Major Obstacle

Indeed, the belief that the current international human rights regime is derived exclusively from the ideological framework of the West is a major obstacle in its acceptance as a truly universal vision. As suggested by a number of human rights scholars, the United Nations must initiate a project to rethink and reformulate the conception of human rights, taking into account the different philosophies that share this planet.

The only way to ensure universal acceptance of and compliance with international human rights law is by removing the crutch used for so long by human rights violators—that human rights as we know it today is a western construct.

Periodical Bibliography

The following articles have been selected to supplement the diverse views presented in this chapter.

Slyvie Bovarnick

"Universal Human Rights and Non-Western Normative Systems: A Comparative Analysis of Violence Against Women in Mexico and Pakistan," *Review of International Studies*, 2007.

Richard Falk

"Human Rights. (Think Again), "*Foreign Policy*, March–April 2007.

Daya Gamage

"Amnesty International's Credibility Challenged: Biased Against Democratic Governments Relative to the Guerrillas," *Asian Tribune*, May 26, 2007.

Zehra F. Kabasakal

"Forging a Global Culture of Human Rights: Origins and Prospects of the International Bill of Rights," *Human Rights Quarterly*, May 2006.

Eric K. Leonard

"Globalization and the Construction of Universal Human Rights," (The History of Human Rights: From Ancient Times to the Globalization Era)(Constructing Human Rights in the Age of Globalization)(Book review). *Human Rights & Human Welfare*, 2006.

Thomas J. Papadimos

"Healthcare Access As a Right, Not a Privilege: A Construct of Western Thought," *Philosophy, Ethics, and Humanities in Medicine*, March 28, 2007.

Randall Peerenbom

"Human Rights, China and Cross-Cultural Inquiry: Philosophy, History and Power Politics," *Philosophy East and West*, May 9, 2007.

Jane Salvage

"Caring in a Forgotten Land: Jane Salvage Visits Turkmenistan, A Central Asian Republic Whose Ruler Shut Every Single Provincial Hospital," *Nursing Standard*, April 5, 2006.

What Is the State
of Human Rights?

Chapter Preface

The last two genocides of the twentieth century occurred in Bosnia and Herzegovina and Rwanda. From 1992 to 1995, some 200,000 Muslims were murdered by Serbs in Bosnia. During 100 days in 1994, some 800,000 Tutsis were slaughtered by the Hutu in Rwanda. These are examples of genocide, a term which means literally "race killing." The term was coined by Polish-Jewish legal scholar Raphael Lemkin after the World War II Holocaust where 6 million Jews were murdered at the hands of the Nazis. Sadly, genocide and other types of government sponsored mass murders have been a common occurrence in the history of humankind, particularly during the twentieth century, and the precise definition of the term "genocide" has become important in human rights law.

The concept of genocide was incorporated into human rights law soon after World War II. Led by the United States, England, and Russia, the world reacted quickly to the atrocities of the Holocaust. First, immediate justice was brought to bear on the top Nazi officials responsible for the atrocities as they were prosecuted in the Nuremberg trials. Then, the world sought to prevent such atrocities from occurring again with the drafting of the Universal Declaration of Human Rights and several human rights treaties. The Convention on the Prevention and Punishment of the Crime of Genocide (CPPCG) was one of the earliest treaties to be adopted by the international community. Lemkin himself put in countless hours lobbying for its adoption. The CPPCG confirms that genocide is a crime under international law whether in times of war or peace and that all signatories agree to prevent it and punish those who violate it. With the Convention on Genocide the world meant to say "never again" to genocide.

Genocide is precisely defined within the CPPCG. Article 2 of the CPPCG says genocide is "any of the following acts committed with intent to destroy, in whole or in part, a national, ethnical, racial or religious group, as such:

(a) Killing members of the group;

(b) Causing serious bodily or mental harm to members of the group;

(c) Deliberately inflicting on the group conditions of life calculated to bring about its physical destruction in whole or in part;

(d) Imposing measures intended to prevent births within the group;

(e) Forcibly transferring children of the group to another group."

The definition of genocide is extremely important in international law. One important impact of the definition is that only crimes against national, ethnical, racial, or religious groups can be called genocide. These are "indelible" groups, since generally an individual is born into the group. The crime of genocide does not apply to the intent to destroy political, ideological, economic, military, professional, or other groups. The rationale generally given for excluding such groups is that one joins or becomes a member of them as a matter of choice, and the nature and membership in such groups is not as clear as it is for indelible groups.

The twentieth century witnessed a shocking number of mass murders, massacres, and slaughters against groups of people. But not all twentieth-century atrocities fit the legal international definition of genocide. The forced deportation and massacre of 2 million Armenians in Turkey from 1915 to 1918 is properly called genocide. So too, is the starvation of 7 million Ukrainians by Soviet leader Joseph Stalin in 1932 to 1933. Of course, the murder of 6 million Jews in the gas chambers of Nazi Germany—having formed the basis for the definition of the term—falls within the definition of genocide. However, the mass murder of perhaps a million or more counterrevolutionaries during the Chinese Cultural Revolution (1966–1969) would not be genocide. Neither would the systematic murder of tens of thousands of communists and leftists by death squads in Latin American from the 1960s to 1980s. Many atrocities occurred in the twentieth century, some of which are called genocide and some of which are not.

The conflict in Darfur, Sudan, which began in 2003, may be the first genocide of the 21st century, or it may not. In September 2006, it was estimated that 200,000 to 400,000 people had been killed and over 2 million displaced from their homes since the crisis began in 2003. Some reports say that the Sudanese government is supporting the rape, murder, and forced displacement of African-Darfurians by generally Arabic Janjaweed militiamen. This interpretation, generally accepted by the United States government and humanitarian organizations, would qualify the Darfur situation as genocide. However, the region's complex ethnic history leads others to a different conclusion. A United Nations report issued in February 2005 found that the attacks by the government and militia forces were indiscriminate in nature and not directed against a particular national, ethnic, racial, or religious group. The report said, "these acts were conducted on a widespread and systematic basis, and therefore may amount to crimes against humanity." However, the report said, "the crucial element of genocidal intent appears to be missing, at least as far as the central government authorities are concerned," and "generally speaking, the policy of attacking, killing and forcibly displacing members of some tribes does not evince a specific intent to annihilate, in whole or in part, a group distinguished on racial, ethnic, national or religious grounds." It remains to be seen how the Darfur crisis will be viewed by history, whether as "just" a crime against humanity or as genocide.

Discussions about the state of human rights are often contentious. No one disputes that atrocities are being committed in Darfur. However, disagreement exists on whether the atrocities meet the legal international definition of genocide. Contention is generally associated with human rights events as they are unfolding, before time and history have had a chance to reflect. In the following chapter the authors debate various issues relevant to the current state of human rights.

> "Neoliberal globalization policies have clearly gone against the spirit and letter of international human rights treaties."

Globalization Threatens Human Rights

Asian Pacific Research Network

In the following viewpoint, the Asian Pacific Research Network (APRN) contends that neoliberal globalization (referring to a "new" set of liberal economic policies that promote the free exchange of goods, services, and cash among nations) violates myriad human rights principles. The APRN cites globalization policies that violate people's rights to work, to food, to health care, and to education. APRN says that the World Trade Organization (WTO), which promotes and regulates globalization, favors the profits of giant transnational corporations at the expense of the human rights of billions of poor people living around the world. The Asian Pacific Research Network is a group of non-governmental organizations that strive to provide information and education on international issues to Asian nations.

Asian Pacific Research Network, "APRN Statement on Human Rights and Trade: The WTO's Decade of Human Rights Violations," *APRN*, December 10, 2005, www.aprnet.org/index.php?a=show&t=issues&i=61. Reproduced by permission.

As you read, consider the following questions:

1. As stated in the viewpoint, what agreement established the World Trade Organization (WTO)? What year was the WTO established?

2. According to the APRN, how many people around the world depend on agricultural production for their livelihoods?

3. According to the APRN, what are three ways the WTO prevents countries from imposing health-promoting policies? What rationale is behind the WTO's prevention of these health-promoting policies?

The rights to food, work, health and education: these are among the most fundamental and inalienable human rights that have systematically been violated as a result of the World Trade Organization [WTO] in its decade of existence. The WTO influences national economic policies which affect the livelihoods and welfare of entire populations. Unfortunately the distorted international trade and investment regime that the WTO is creating, reflected in national economic policies, is one that systematically fails to consider the real development needs of the underdeveloped countries and their peoples.

Millions of people in the world's vast underdeveloped countries have already suffered, arguably making the WTO an instrument for human rights violations of epic proportions. If human rights "economic, political, social, civil and cultural" are not placed at the heart of negotiations on international trade and investment pacts, not only will these millions continue to suffer but they will even be joined by so many millions more.

Globalization Violates Human Rights Principles

The central problem is that the WTO systematically disregards human rights: its core philosophy of neoliberal "globalization" is methodically biased for "free" trade that promotes corporate monopoly profits rather than human well-being and development; the big developed country governments aggressively push anti-developmental economic policies, which underdeveloped country governments tolerate and indeed sometimes even embrace. The end result is that domestic productive and social welfare structures around the world are devastated with severe effects especially on the economically vulnerable parts of populations who are the most numerous.

And yet almost all of the WTO's member states have obligations under international human rights treaties and conventions that legally bind them to respect, recognize, uphold and promote human rights. This means that the trade and investment pacts they enter into, and the national economic policies that they implement, cannot violate the human rights either of their citizens or of those of other nations.

The norms of international human rights law are well-developed and, spanning nearly six decades, long pre-date the merely decade-old WTO. Human rights were definitively established as early as the Charter of the United Nations (UN) that even the WTO has to recognize. Consequently, Article XVI, paragraph 6 of the Marrakesh Agreement Establishing the WTO (15 April, 1994) says: This Agreement shall be registered in accordance with the provisions of Article 102 of the Charter of the United Nations. Article 102 of the UN Charter governs treaties and international agreements entered into by UN Member States, hence the WTO is a membership organization unambiguously founded under the Charter of the United Nations.

Human rights were subsequently fleshed out further, beginning with the 1948 Universal Declaration of Human Rights (UDHR) and the UN Declaration on the Right to Development. Specific rights were identified and elaborated in the twin 1966 treaties of the International Covenant on Civil and Political Rights (ICCPR) and the International Covenant on

Economic Social and Cultural Rights (ICESCR). The UDHR, ICCPR, and ICESCR constitute a virtually international bill of human rights. Further emphasis and clarification of norms were made through the Convention on the Rights of the Child (CRC) and the Convention on the Elimination of All Forms of Discrimination Against Women (CEDAW).

This is a body of international human rights jurisprudence that cannot be disregarded by the international trade and investment law being laid down by the WTO and, indeed, must take precedence insofar as trade and investment are merely means to development ends. WTO member states must above all uphold their international human rights and treaty obligations.

Consequently, international economic policy forums such as the WTO must not be used in ways that actively violate the human rights of peoples. And more than that, they should even be actively used to enable governments to discharge their human rights obligations to their peoples.

WTO Favors Giant Corporations

The WTO, however, has done the exact opposite in its decade of existence and has pushed neoliberal "globalization" policies—one-sidedly at that—to the detriment of the most numerous and most vulnerable sectors of society. The main subjects and ultimate beneficiaries of the WTO's free market policies have been giant transnational corporations (TNCs) and countries' political and economic elites rather than the countless individual human beings most in need.

It has ever more geared the world's economic policies towards promoting corporate and elite profits: the underdeveloped countries have been opened up to foreign trade and investment even as the protections and support for rich country TNCs continue. This has worsened poverty, deepened inequality and prevented the progressive realization of the human rights of billions.

Concerns About Globalization

The achievements of the era of globalization should not blind us to the new anxieties that globalization has brought in its wake. The reach of globalization is yet to touch many parts of the world. Moreover, the evidence suggests that the process has not removed personal and regional income disparities. In many developing countries, growth is by-passing the rural areas. Also, in the face of stagnation in their real pay, the working classes in industrialized countries are becoming fearful of the opening of markets. The gap between the rich and the poor is widening. This, coupled with the inability of the public sector to provide adequate and quality services in health and education, and cater to the needs of the poor, is causing resentment and alienation. This is nurturing divisive forces and putting pressure on the practice of democracy.

Manmohan Singh, Prime Minister of India,
Address at Cambridge University, October 11, 2006,
The Hindu, www.hindunet.com.

WTO Violates People's Right to Work and to Food

The WTO violates people's right to work and to food. Nearly three billion people around the world, overwhelmingly in the underdeveloped countries, directly depend on agricultural production for their livelihoods. Yet the WTO's Agreement on Agriculture (AoA) has been used to tear down tariff and non-tariff barriers in the underdeveloped countries while permitting the developed countries to maintain billions of dollars in agricultural subsidies. This lop-sided agricultural trade has deprived millions of people of the most basic means for survival.

Cheap agricultural imports have flooded underdeveloped country markets, destroyed rural livelihoods, and displaced millions of farmers and farmworkers. As it is, some 750 million people worldwide are unemployed or otherwise still not earning enough from the work they have and are looking for more work. The collapse of domestic food production and the lost incomes of rural producers combine to drive people into hunger. A billion people are hungry every day of which 200 million are malnourished children under 5 years.

Trade liberalization has also intensified the process of workers being pitted against each other, and of their wages and benefits being driven down in a race to the bottom in the name of increased corporate competitiveness. Even the working people of the developed countries have been adversely affected.

WTO Violates People's Right to Health

The WTO violates people's right to health. On one hand, there are the adverse health outcomes due to lost livelihoods and deepening poverty. Health has become a luxury good for the 2.8 billion people, or over half the world's population of 6.4 billion, who are miserably poor and struggle to survive on US$2 or less each day. Two billion people do not even have safe water to drink. Each year as a result of all this, 25 million men, women and children die from hunger and curable diseases. Half a million women die in pregnancy and childbirth. In the poorest countries more than one in four children die before they are 5 years old.

But the WTO also directly attacks people's health in the interests of corporate monopoly profits. Despite the supposed solution on the agreement on Trade-Related Intellectual Property Rights (TRIPS) and public health, the world's poor still do not have access to affordable drugs. Underdeveloped countries without pharmaceutical manufacturing capacity have difficulty to import cheap generic drugs to address public health problems such as HIV/AIDS, and manufacturers of generic drugs are still unable to supply them because of stringent international patent protection rules. The TRIPS agreement also lays the basis for monopoly control, for profit, of indigenous knowledge that has been around for hundreds of years by creating the opportunity for giant TNCs to patent and control this knowledge.

The WTO also disarms countries from imposing health-promoting but allegedly trade-distorting measures such as banning the entry of genetically engineered foods and seeds, or promoting mother's breast milk over prepared infant formulas to reduce infant mortality, or stopping the import of unsafe materials like asbestos, and so on.

The intensified negotiations on the General Agreement on Trade in Services (GATS) will also have severe consequences. The GATS will erode government's power to regulate profit-seeking foreign investment in important public utilities, such as water and sanitation, and in vital social services, such as health and education. This will grossly undermine the ability of governments to meet their commitments under various human rights treaties to make these services affordable and accessible to all its citizens.

WTO Violates People's Right to Education

The WTO violates people's right to education. For the world's poor and increasingly poor, education is, like health, ever more a luxury good beyond their consumption. Educational systems around the world are decrepit or otherwise unafford-able. Over 20 percent of children do not even finish primary school and one in five adults is illiterate. The GATS especially as currently being negotiated [as of 2005] will only make this situation worse.

At the same time, the WTO conveniently turns a blind eye to people's right to safety and security. While the WTO attacks people's livelihoods and welfare it protects the big powers' war industries through the General Agreement on Tariffs and Trade (GATT) Article XXI security exception. About a trillion dollars are spent annually in the global arms race of which half is of the United States' (US) alone. All these weapons of mass destruction while, grotesquely, billions of people are denied food, work, health and education.

Globalization Violates Human Rights Treaties

The vast majority of humanity suffers the ills of poverty and is mired in hunger, disease and ignorance. Trade and investment policies have a direct and immediate impact on these and cannot be negotiated without taking international human rights obligations fully into account and be guided by these principles. Indeed, trade and investment policies must not just pay attention to human rights but precisely be about actively promoting economic and social rights to food, work, education and health. The welfare of billions cannot be left to the dictates of the free market, self-serving political elites and big business.

Neoliberal globalization policies have clearly gone against the spirit and letter of international human rights treaties. The advanced powers have used the WTO, International Monetary Fund (IMF) and World Bank (WB) to aggressively push tight fiscal and monetary policies, open trade and investment regimes, and the right of corporations to make their monopoly profits. At the same time they restrict access to their domestic markets and continue giving their TNCs special privileges and subsidies. The world's enormous numbers of poor that are most economically vulnerable have suffered greatly from these.

There must be a halt to new international economic policy agreements, and to greater liberalization through revisions in existing agreements, while the human rights impact of current agreements are assessed. All governments must uphold the primacy of international human rights law and human development. In both the review of existing international trade and investment rules and in the negotiation of future rules, they must be accountable to their binding human rights obligations.

There must be an immediate change in the national economic policies that are seen to breed the conditions for human rights violations, including an effective halt to the implementation of the relevant international agreements.

There must be a comprehensive review of the WTO's policies and rules towards ensuring that whatever international trade and investment policies are advanced will be consistent with existing treaties, legislation and policies designed to protect and promote all human rights. International trade, investment and finance are not exempt from human rights principles—indeed they must be formulated to ensure that the greatest number, and in particular the most vulnerable sectors, enjoy fundamental human rights such as to food, work, health, education and housing.

There must be an international trade and investment regime that upholds economic sovereignty, especially the right of nations to take all the measures they deem necessary to protect and promote the human rights of their citizens. A multilateral forum that denies this does not have any moral and political legitimacy, and neither do the governments supporting such a forum. Powerful geopolitical and economic minorities must not be allowed to dominate or dictate procedures, processes and decision-making.

The current world economic order dominated by big power governments and their monopoly TNCs is a world where people's lives are constantly and rapidly getting worse. Among the most urgent steps we can take in working towards a more secure, equitable, and prosperous place for everyone is to make sure that human rights are central to the scope, content and process of all international trade and investment negotiations.

> "For the past three decades, globaliza-
> tion, human rights, and democracy
> have been marching forward together,
> haltingly, not always and everywhere
> in step, but in a way that unmistak-
> ably shows they are interconnected."

Globalization Promotes Human Rights

Daniel T. Griswold

*In the following viewpoint, Michael Griswold argues that global-
ization leads to freedom, democracy, and respect for human
rights. Griswold says that globalization empowers people, makes
them less dependent on governments for their livelihood, more
politically aware, and less accepting of government human rights
violations. Furthermore, when governments allow their citizens
to participate in the global economy it becomes harder for them
to deny civil and political human rights. Daniel Griswold is director of the Center for Trade Policy Studies at the Cato Institute
in Washington, D.C.*

Daniel T. Griswold, "Globalization, Human Rights, and Democracy," *eJournalUSA:
Global Issues*, February 2006, http://usinfo.state.gov/journals/itgic/0206/ijge/
griswold.htm.

As you read, consider the following questions:

1. What is the "CNN effect," according to Griswold?
2. According to a survey by the human rights organization, Freedom House, the number of people in the world that are "free" has increased by how much in the last three decades?
3. Name ten countries where Griswold says political reforms have followed economic reforms.

When trade and globalization are discussed in the U.S. Congress and in the American media, the focus is almost entirely on the economic impact at home—on manufacturing, jobs, and wages. But trade is about more than exporting soybeans and machine tools. It is also about exporting freedom and democracy.

Since September 11, 2001, the [George W.] Bush administration has articulated the argument that trade can and must play a role in promoting democracy and human rights in the rest of the world. In an April 2002 speech, President Bush said, "Trade creates the habits of freedom," and those habits "begin to create the expectations of democracy and demands for better democratic institutions. Societies that are open to commerce across their borders are more open to democracy within their borders."

Globalization Can Empower People

The connection between trade, development, and political reform is not just a throwaway line. In theory and in practice, economic and political freedoms reinforce one another. Political philosophers from Aristotle to Samuel Huntington have noted that economic development and an expanding middle class can provide more fertile ground for democracy.

Trade and globalization can spur political reform by expanding the freedom of people to exercise greater control over their daily lives. In less developed countries, the expansion of markets means they no longer need to bribe or beg government officials for permission to import a television set or spare parts for their tractor. Controls on foreign exchange no longer limit their freedom to travel abroad. They can more easily acquire tools of communication such as mobile phones, Internet access, satellite TV, and fax machines.

As workers and producers, people in more open countries are less dependent on the authorities for their livelihoods. For example, in a more open, market-driven economy, the government can no longer deprive independent newspapers of newsprint if they should displease the ruling authorities. In a more open economy and society, the "CNN effect" of global media and consumer attention exposes and discourages the abuse of workers. Multinational companies have even greater incentives to offer competitive benefits and wages in more globalized developing countries than in those that are closed.

Economic freedom and rising incomes, in turn, help to nurture a more educated and politically aware middle class. A rising business class and wealthier civil society create leaders and centers of influence outside government. People who are economically free over time want and expect to exercise their political and civil rights as well. In contrast, a government that can seal its citizens off from the rest of the world can more easily control them and deprive them of the resources and information they could use to challenge its authority.

Globalization Tied to Democracy and Freedom

As theory would predict, trade, development, and political and civil freedom appear to be tied together in the real world. Everyone can agree that the world is more globalized than it was 30 years ago, but less widely appreciated is the fact that the world is much more democratized than it was 30 years ago. According to the most recent survey by Freedom House, the share of the world's population enjoying full political and civil freedoms has increased substantially in the past three decades, as has the share of the world's governments that are democratic.

In its annual survey, released in December 2005, the human rights research organization reported that 46 percent of the world's population now lives in countries it classifies as "Free," where citizens "enjoy open political competition, a climate of respect for civil liberties, significant independent civic life, and independent media." That compares to the 35 percent of mankind that enjoyed a similar level of freedom in 1973. The percentage of people in countries that are "Not Free," where political and civil liberties are systematically oppressed, dropped during the same period from 47 percent to 36 percent. The percentage of the population in countries that are "Partly Free" has remained at 18 percent. Meanwhile, the percentage of the world's governments that are democracies has reached 64 percent, the highest in the 33 years of Freedom House surveys.

Thanks in good measure to the liberating winds of globalization, the shift of 11 percentage points of the world's population in the past three decades from "Not Free" to "Free" means that another 650 million human beings today enjoy the kind of civil and political liberties taken for granted in such countries as the United States, Japan, and Belgium, instead of suffering under the kind of tyranny we still see in the most repressive countries.

Within individual countries, economic and political freedoms also appear to be linked. A 2004 study by the Cato Institute, titled *"Trading Tyranny for Freedom,"* found that countries that are relatively open to the global economy are much more likely to be democracies that respect civil and political liberties than those that are relatively closed. And relatively closed countries are far more likely to deny systematically civil and political liberties than those that are open.

Countries that Have Benefitted from Globalization

- **China:** Reform led to the largest poverty reduction in history. The number of rural poor fell from 250 million in 1978 to 34 million in 1999.

- **India:** Cut its poverty rate in half in the past two decades.

- **Uganda:** Poverty fell 40% during the 1990s and school enrollments doubled.

- **Vietnam:** Surveys of the country's poorest households show 98% of people improved their living conditions in the 1990s. The government conducted a household survey at the beginning of reforms and went back 6 years later to the same households and found impressive reductions in poverty. People had more food to eat and children were attending secondary school. Trade liberalization was one factor among many that contributed to Vietnam's success. The country cut poverty in half in a decade. Economic integration raised the prices for the products of poor farmers—rice, fish, cashews— and also created large numbers of factory jobs in footwear and garments, jobs that paid a lot more than existing opportunities in Vietnam.

Youthink! The WorldBank,
www.youthink.worldbank.org.

Economic Freedom Can Lead to Political Reform

In the past two decades, a number of economies have followed the path of economic and trade reform leading to political reform. South Korea and Taiwan as recently as the 1980s were governed by authoritarian regimes that did not permit much open dissent. Today, after years of expanding trade and rising incomes, both are multiparty democracies with full political and civil liberties. Other countries that have most aggressively followed those twin tracks of reform include Chile, Ghana, Hungary, Mexico, Nicaragua, Paraguay, Portugal, and Tanzania.

In other words, governments that grant their citizens a large measure of freedom to engage in international commerce find it increasingly difficult to deprive them of political and civil liberties, while governments that "protect" their citizens behind tariff walls and other barriers to international commerce find it much easier to deny those same liberties. Of course, the correlation between economic openness and political freedom across countries is not perfect, but the broad trends are undeniable.

The application for U.S. foreign policy is that trade and development, along with its economic benefits, can prove to be powerful tools for spreading broader freedoms and democracy around the world.

Globalization Can Promote Human Rights

In mainland China, for example, economic reform and globalization give reason to hope for political reforms. After 25 years of reform and rapid growth, an expanding middle class is experiencing for the first time the independence of home ownership, travel abroad, and cooperation with others in economic enterprise free of government control. The number of telephone lines, mobile phones, and Internet users has risen exponentially in the past decade. Millions of Chinese students and tourists travel abroad each year. That can only be good news for individual freedom in China, and a growing problem for the government.

Free trade and globalization can also play a role in promoting democracy and human rights in the Middle East. In a

May 2003 address outlining his plan for a Middle East free trade area, President Bush said, "The Arab world has a great cultural tradition, but is largely missing out on the economic progress of our time. Across the globe, free markets and trade have helped defeat poverty, and taught men and women the habits of liberty."

Economic stagnation in the Middle East feeds terrorism, not because of poverty but because of a lack of opportunity and hope for a better future, especially among the young. Young people who cannot find meaningful work and who cannot participate in the political process are ripe pickings for religious fanatics and terrorist recruiters. Any effort to encourage greater freedom in the Middle East must include an agenda for promoting economic liberty and openness.

Globalization Interconnected with Human Rights

On a multilateral level, a successful agreement through the World Trade Organization (WTO) would create a more friendly climate globally for democracy and human rights. Less developed countries, by opening up their own, relatively closed markets and gaining greater access to rich-country markets, could achieve higher rates of growth and develop the expanding middle class that forms the backbone of most democracies. A successful conclusion of the WTO Doha Development Round of trade negotiations that began in 2001 would reinforce the twin trends of globalization and the spread of political and civil liberties that have marked the last 30 years. Failure would delay and frustrate progress on both fronts for millions of people.

For the past three decades, globalization, human rights, and democracy have been marching forward together, haltingly, not always and everywhere in step, but in a way that unmistakably shows they are interconnected. By encouraging globalization in less developed countries, we not only help to raise growth rates and incomes, promote higher standards, and feed, clothe, and house the poor; we also spread political and civil freedoms.

"Islamic Sharia law should be opposed by everyone who believes in universal human rights, women's civil rights and individual freedom."

Islamic Law Threatens Human Rights

Azam Kamguian

In the following viewpoint, Azam Kamguian argues against the establishment of Islamic tribunals in Canada and contends that Sharia law, that is, traditional Islamic law, is antithetical to human rights. Kamguian lays out her case against Sharia law, saying it opposes human rights, women's rights, freedom of expression, and freedom of religion. Kamguian calls for an end to Canadian Islamic tribunals and the establishment of secular states and societies. Azam Kamguian is the chairperson of the Committee to Defend Women's Rights in the Middle East.

As you read, consider the following questions:

1. According to Kamguian, which countries suppress people's rights and freedoms, particularly women's, under the movement called "political Islam"?

Azam Kamguian, "Islamism & Multi-Culturalism: A United Camp Against Universal Human Rights in Canada," *Adapted from the speech "The Sharia Courts & Women's Rights in Canada,"* March 7, 2004. www.middleastwomen.org/html/multi.htm.

2. Kamguian says the Sharia only reflects the social and economic conditions of what time in Islamic history?

3. What message does Kamguian say is being sent (and to whom) when religion is accepted as a justification for human rights abuses?

Sharia Law in the West

As we all know, Islamists in Canada have recently [as of 2004] set up an Islamic Institute of Civil Justice to oversee tribunals that would arbitrate family disputes and other civil matters between people from Muslim origin on the basis of the Islamic Sharia law. This is the first time in any western country that the medieval precepts of the Sharia have been given any validity. One can imagine that the Islamists will use this as a lever to work for similar recognition in many other western countries. After all, if Canada is prepared to recognise Sharia law in this way why not every other country in the west.

This move is yet another effort by Islamists to impose the barbaric Sharia law, but this time on the people in the west. This move belongs to political Islam, a major force that has brutally suppressed people's rights and freedom in general and women's rights in particular in the Middle East. It is a political movement that came to the fore against the secular and progressive movements for liberation and egalitarianism in the Middle East. In Iran, the Sudan, Pakistan and Afghanistan, Islamic regimes proceeded to transform women's homes into prison houses, where confinement of women, their exclusion from many fields of work and education, and their brutal treatment became the law of the land.

Multi-Culturalism Causes Racism, Suits Islamists

Sadly and unfortunately, the setting up of the Sharia tribunals in Canada will be given validity, due to the reactionary politics of multi-culturalism. This is yet another fruit of a policy that causes fragmentation; apartheid based legal system and racism. Of course, this politics of fragmentation and apartheid suits the purpose of Islamists best. Mr. Mohamed El Masry, president of the Canadian Islamic Congress, has argued that Canada needs "a multiplicity of laws" to accommodate different groups when their moral standards clash. Mr. El Masry says the tribunals, which would include imams, elders and lawyers, will provide Muslims with the means to settle civil disputes out of court according to their beliefs.

Advocates for the Islamic tribunals have argued that one of the beauties of free and open societies in the west is their flexibility. But the very same "flexibility" provides the Islamists with the opportunity to impose their own rigid and oppressive rules on a specific community in the society. Mr. Momtaz Ali, president of the Canadian Society of Muslims and a leading proponent of the Islamic tribunals, has said: "It—the Islamic tribunal—offers not only a variety of choices, but shows the real spirit of our multicultural society," The very same Mr. Ali also says: "On religious grounds, a Muslim who would choose to opt out . . . would be guilty of a far greater crime than a mere breach of contract—and this would be tantamount to blasphemy or apostasy". You are aware that blasphemy and apostasy are among the worst crimes in Islam, in many countries punishable by death.

This project is against the equality of all citizens before the law, regardless of race, religion or gender. Such equality does not exist under the Islamic Sharia law. Sharia tribunals effectively establish a parallel legal system based on religion, which I believe will lead to an apartheid-based legal system. The principles of individual freedom and equality before the law should take precedence over any collective goals that members of a particular group might claim for themselves.

Women Subjugated in Islamic Society

In order to protect their morality women can have no contact with men to whom they are not related without the presence of a male relative. The segregation of sexes in this way makes it very difficult for women to leave their houses and participate in society in any way at all. Under the Taliban many war widows were forced into starvation. Their crime? Had they prayed harder their husbands would have survived!

Many apologists for Islam, women among them, argue that women are happy in their roles in Islamic society, happy to be afforded the protection of their menfolk and to be kept away from the gaze of other men. But this of course is a false argument. If some women want to stay at home under the protection of their men they can do so. But do the apologists for Islam have the right to tell all other women, including non-Muslims, how they should behave? Women deserve to be treated as autonomous human beings and for this reason alone misogynistic Political Islam and its imposition of the Sharia should be opposed.

"No to Political Islam Campaign,"
www.ntpi.org, 22 September 2004.

Sharia Law Harms Women

Many people from Muslim origin will be pressured into accepting arbitration by the Islamic Institute on matters of civil and family law. This presents a serious problem for the rights of particularly women living in Canada. The decisions of the tribunal will be final and binding and will be upheld by the Canadian courts. The Institute will be applying Islamic Sharia law which is totally against impartiality of the legal systems. For example, a woman's testimony under the Sharia counts only as half that of a man. So in straight disagreements between husband and wife, the husband's testimony will normally prevail. In questions of inheritance, whilst under Canadian law sons and daughters would be treated equally, under the Sharia daughters receive only half the portion of sons. If the Institute were to have jurisdiction in custody cases, the man will automatically be awarded custody once the children have reached an age of between seven and nine years. Given this inequality it is particularly worrying that there will be no right of appeal to the Canadian courts. The principle being that if both parties in a dispute willingly submit to Islamic arbitration, they can't complain when they lose.

The problem here is the word "willing". Too many women from Muslim origin living in the west still live in Islamic and patriarchal environments where the man's word and pressure from the community is law. It will take a brave woman to defy her husband, and to refuse to have her dispute settled under Islamic law when her refusal could be equated with hostility to the religion and apostasy. To this is added the problem that going to a Canadian court will take longer and cost more. There is no reason, however, why arbitration service under Canadian law could not be used instead. The danger is that once these tribunals are set up people from Muslim origin will be pressured to use them, thereby being deprived of many of the rights that people in the west have fought for for centuries.

Religion Not Separate

In virtually every western country with a sizeable Muslim minority there is pressure from Islamists for a separate civil and criminal law. They seek to establish their own state to oppress people, legally and officially. There must be no state within a state. Yet this is precisely the objective that the Islamic advocates are pursuing. They argue that it is their duty as good Muslims to work for precisely this end. And this end precisely leads to more forced marriages, more honour killings, more

Islamic schools, more FGM-s [female genital mutilation] done secretly, and more harassment and intimidation towards women and girls in ghettos.

In Islam, as Mr. Momtaz Ali has said, there is no separation between religion and the law. But in the contemporary civilisation, laws are seen as the work of man and as such can be changed in the light of changing circumstances. In Islam, the law is against universal women and human rights, but is God's law, and change is impossible.

Sharia Law Antithetical to Human Rights

Islamic Sharia law should be opposed by everyone who believes in universal human rights, women's civil rights and individual freedom, freedom of expression, freedom of religion and belief freedom from religion. Islamic law developed in the first few centuries of Islam and incorporated Middle Eastern pre-Islamic misogynist and tribal customs and traditions. We may ask how a law whose elements were first laid down over 1,000 years ago can be relevant in the 21st century. The Sharia only reflects the social and economic conditions of the time of Abbasid and has grown out of touch with all the human's social, economic, cultural and moral developments. The principles of the Sharia are inimical to human's moral progress and civilised values.

Islamic law forcefully opposes free thought, freedom of expression and freedom of action. Accusations of impurity, of apostasy are waiting to silence any voice of dissent. Suppression and injustice shapes the lives of all free minded people. One is borne and labelled Muslim, and one is forced to stay Muslim to the end of their life. Islamic law denies the rights of women and non-Muslim religious minorities. Non-believers are shown no tolerance: death or conversion. Jews and Christians are treated as second-class citizens.

Under the Sharia, for over two decades, millions around the world have fallen victim: countless people have been executed, beheaded, stoned to death, had their limbs cut off, flogged and maimed, bombed to pieces and routed. In countries which have proclaimed an Islamic state, such as Iran, the Sudan, Pakistan, some states in Northern Nigeria, and Afghanistan, we have already seen the pernicious effects of the Sharia.

Human rights and the Sharia are definitely and irremediably irreconcilable and antagonistic. Universal human rights are essential to ensure a certain standard of living for people across the globe. It is not acceptable to let governments and authorities away with many of the abuses by using multiculturalism as an excuse. We cannot let multiculturalism become the last refuge of repression. To accept religion as a justification for human rights abuses is to discriminate against the abused and to send the message that they are undeserving of human rights protection.

Secular State Needed

Multiculturalism is a cover to create a comprehensive social, legal, intellectual, emotional, and civil apartheid based on distinctions of race, ethnicity, religion and gender. This complete system of apartheid attacks women's basic rights and freedom and justifies misogynist rule inflicted on women by Islamists. Any attempt to restrict human and women's rights in the name of religion and culture, or defining freedom and equality according to different cultures and religions is racist.

Our contemporary society is far larger, diverse and complex than the small primitive tribal society in Arabia, 1,400 years ago, from which Islam emerged. It is time to abandon the idea that anyone should live under the Sharia. More than ever before, people need a secular state as well as a secular society that respects freedom from and of religion, and human rights founded on the principle that power belongs to the people and not to God. It is crucial to oppose the Islamic Sharia law and to subordinate Islam to secularism and secular states.

I call upon all secularist forces and freedom-lovers to stand up and protest against the setting up of Islamic tribunals in Canada. All progressive people should make a joint effort to stop Islamism and multicultural politics of the Canadian authorities from violating the universal human rights and our civilised values.

| "Yes, Islam has a place for human rights."

Islamic Law Promotes Human Rights

Louay M. Safi

In this viewpoint, a question and answer session, Louay Safi claims that human rights are important in Islamic law. Safi tackles questions from the audience regarding the position of Islamic law in relation to corporal punishment, equality, women's rights, freedom of speech, and freedom of religion. Safi contends that several Islamic principles protect human rights and the Qur'an or Koran—the religious text of Islam—declares the equality of all human beings. Dr. Louay M. Safi serves as the executive director of ISNA Leadership Development Center, Indianapolis, Indiana. He writes and lectures on issues relating to Islam, American Muslims, democracy, human rights, leadership, and world peace. He is the author of eight books and numerous papers, including Tensions and Transitions in the Muslim World, *published by University Press of America, 2003.*

As you read, consider the following questions:

1. Safi says there is confusion in the West about the importance of human rights in Islam because of

Louay M. Safi, "Question and Answer Session: Prophet Muhammad & Human Rights," *www.islamonline.net*, April 20, 2006. Reproduced by permission of the author.

the way some people promote human rights. What examples of this does he give?

2. What is the helfaul-madinah? Name three of its provisions that Safi says promotes human rights.

3. According to Safi, does the Qur'an guarantee equal rights to non-Muslims?

Question: Do you mean that Islam has a place for human rights?

Answer: Yes, Islam has a place for human rights. We need to remember that human rights are intended to protect the dignity of human beings. This was the mission of the Prophet of Islam (peace and blessings be upon him). God Almighty summarized his mission as thus: "We sent you as a mercy to humanity." (Al-Hajj 22: 107)

The confusion about the importance of human rights in Islam is often derived from the way certain groups in the West promote human rights. On the one hand there are those who use human rights as a tool to reject non-western traditions, and therefore promote certain social ills, such as same-sex relations under the banner of human rights. There are also those who use human rights selectively to justify western intervention in the internal affairs of Muslim societies. But human rights are not about these practices, they are about, as I indicated, ensuring the well-being of humanity, and this is the intention and the purpose of revelation.

Muslims need to develop human rights traditions on the basis of Islamic values and principles. And when they do that the apparent contradiction will disappear.

Question: Islam stipulates corporal punishments; does not this represent a violation for human rights?

Answer: Punishments are prescribed to deter criminal behavior and protect society from the actions of immoral persons. Corporal punishments that were historically prescribed by Islamic Shari'ah were not intended to cause physical harm, but to rebuke those individuals who are caught committing crimes. That is why Prophet Muhammad repeatedly directed Muslims to apply such punishments in a mild way so that the physical harm is prevented.

We should also note that corporal punishments within Islamic traditions are often provided as the upper limitation on acceptable penalty, and combined with alternative means for fighting crimes, and therefore, there are other options to be used which would allow the community to reserve corporal punishment as a means of last resort.

Question: What are the basic principles that make up the Islamic perspective on human rights?

Answer: There are a number of principles that form the foundation of human rights tradition in Islam, foremost among which is the Qur'anic declaration of the equality of human beings. One reads, for example, in Chapter 49, verse 13: "O mankind, we have created you from a single pair of a male and female, and made you into nations and tribes so that you may recognize one another; the most honored of you in the sight of Allah is the most righteous of you." (Al-Hujurat 49: 13)

Another central principle is the freedom of consciousness that is the right of people to follow their own convictions. Again the Qur'an asserts that there should be no compulsion in matters of faith, as the Qur'an stresses in Chapter 2: "Let there be no compulsion in religion; truth stands out clear from error." (Al-Baqarah 2: 255)

Prophet Muhammad (peace and blessings be upon him), has translated the various Islamic principles that protect human rights in the covenant that he entered to with the various tribes of Medina, better known as sahifatul-madinah. This covenant includes a number of provisions that precede any known documents promoting human rights. This includes, for example, freedom of belief; "the Jews have their religion and the Muslim theirs"; freedom of movement from and to Medina; "whoever will go out is safe, and whoever will stay in Medina is safe"; or outlawing guilt by association which was commonly practiced by the pre-Islamic Arab tribes; "the person is not liable for his allies' misdeeds."

Question: Could you please elaborate on how Islam preserved human rights keeping into consideration the status quo of Muslims?

Answer: It is clear that in many Muslim societies today we observe frequent violations of human rights. These include lack of freedom of expression and, therefore, the difficulties in fighting corruption, particularly state corruption. It is the duty of all Muslims to promote the common good and to prevent corruption in society. This is the essence of the principle of enjoining what is good and forbidding what is evil.

Muslims today must develop ways and means to be able to work together to ensure the right and the ability of citizens to point out any wrong doings and safeguard the public good.

Question: How did the Prophet (peace be upon him) approve women's right to equality with men?

Answer: It was the Qur'an that clearly established the principle of spiritual and social equality between men and women. Spiritual equality is quite evident in Chapter 33, verse 35, in which the Qur'an refers to the two genders when calling the believers to uphold to the spiritual requirements of Islam. Similarly, in Chapter 9, verse 71 the Qur'an declares the believing men and women as protectors and helpers of one another "awliya." It goes on to say, "they collaborate to promote all what is good and oppose all that is evil."

This is obviously an obligation to safeguard the public space, which means that women also have an obligation to promote public good and to prevent corruption in the public.

The Qur'an refers to complementary responsibilities for men and women with regard to family matters. It is here where early scholars have assigned different rights and responsibilities for men and women, but here we have to realize that these differences are about allowing the two genders to complement one another, and it should not be used to provide privileges to one gender or deny the other gender their human dignity that God has given all human beings.

Question: One of the well-established human rights is freedom of religion. Then, how Prophet Muhammad (peace be upon him) did assure this right, when he said in a hadith that one who changes his religion is to be killed?

Answer: It is true that there are some reported hadiths calling for capital punishments for individuals who change their religion. But these hadiths must be understood in relation to others hadiths and practices of the Prophet, and in relation to Qur'anic verses. The Qur'an is quite clear that human beings have freedom of religion; have the freedom to accept revelation or to reject it as long as they do not cause harm to others, as we find in the following verses: 2: 256, 10:99, 11:28, 17:84, and others.

We also know that the Prophet did pardon Abdullah Ibn Sa'd who committed apostasy and later on was brought to him by his cousin, 'Uthman Ibn 'Affan, who interceded on his behalf. This tradition of the Prophet, peace be upon him, leads us to believe that the other two hadiths relate to individuals who change their religion and commit an act of treason and rebellion against the community. This is in keeping with the commonly held interpretation that apostasy involves acts of armed rebellion and not simply a quiet change of religion.

Question: I understand that your religion guarantee human rights for Muslims, but what about to non-Muslims? Are they guaranteed equal rights? Could you give examples, if any, of the Prophet's handling of this issue?

Answer: Indeed Islam recognized the human rights of all people. As I indicated earlier, the prophet of Islam did recognize the right to religious freedom and equal protection with regard to Jewish tribes of Medina. He did that in keeping with the teachings of the Qur'an that require Muslims to deal with people of other faiths with respect. The Qur'an, for example, asks Muslims to dialogue with the People of Book in the best of manners.

Question: What is the stance of Islam on the freedom of speech?

Answer: Islam protects freedom of speech, particularly when it is intended to speaking out against abuse of power and corruption. In fact Islam bestows a great honor and reward for a person who speaks out against unjust authorities. However, freedom of expression should not be confused with the freedom to slander, to promote lies and character assassination, and those who fabricate stories to defame other individuals and groups should be held liable, should be responsible for their actions.

Question: How Muhammad viewed concept of justice and equality?

Answer: Justice is at the core of Islamic revelation. Indeed, the Qur'an declares that justice or al-qist is the purpose for revealing Divine Books to humanity. As we read in surat al-hadeed: "We sent aforetime Our Messengers with Clear Signs and sent down with them the Book and the Balance (of Right and Wrong), that people may stand forth in justice." (Al-Hadeed 25: 58)

The Qur'an even asks Muslims to be just with their foes and enemies: "O ye who believe! stand out firmly for Allah, as witnesses to fair dealing, and let not the hatred of others to you make you swerve to wrong and depart from justice. Be just: that is next to Piety: and fear Allah. For Allah is well-acquainted with all that ye do." (Al-Ma'idah 5: 8)

The Prophet adhered closely to the Qur'anic teachings, and there are numerous examples that we find when we read his biographies. The Prophet, peace be upon him, insisted on dealing with all with peace and equity as we see in his directives to the Muslims to apply law equally to the poor and notables in the community: "O people, those who came before you received divine punishment because they let go the wealthy people who committed acts of robbery while administered the punishment for the poor. By Allah, if Fatimah, the daughter of Muhammad, were to commit robbery, Muhammad would cut her hand."

Question: You said your prophet repeatedly directed Muslims to apply such punishments in a mild way so that the physical harm is prevented. Where is that mild way in cutting off the hand of the thief?

Answer: Cutting the hands of the thief should be understood within the conditions that have been outlined by Muslim scholars. One of the conditions for cutting the hands is that theft should have taken place in a locked and inhabited house. In other words, the acts of the thief would endanger the lives of people who inhabit the house, and that justifies providing a severe punishment that will deter potential thieves.

An act of theft which takes place in an uninhabited house, or affects unprotected properties, is not punishable by cutting the hands. In other words, this issue from an Islamic point of view must be considered with regard to the extent to which the act of theft can endanger and can possibly lead to the loss of human life.

Question: What about slavery in Islam?

Answer: Islam has taken every opportunity to free slaves. For example, there are many occasions where freeing a slave is the way to expiate one's wrongdoings. Therefore, I can say without any hesitation that slavery has no place in Islam. As it was well put in the words of 'Umar Ibn Al-Khattab, the second caliph of Islam: "how would you enslave people when their mothers brought them free to this life."

Question: Could you please clarify in unequivocal terms the position of Islam on terrorism? Does Islam allow such appalling attacks made in the name of Islam by some Muslims?

The Qu'ran: Magna Carta of Human Rights

Given the centrality of the Qur'an to the lives of the majority of the more than one billion Muslims of the world, the critical question is: What, if anything, does the Qur'an say about human rights? I believe that the Qur'an is the Magna Carta of human rights and that a large part of its concern is to free human beings from the bondage of traditionalism, authoritarianism (religious, political, economic, or any other), tribalism, racism, sexism, slavery or anything else that prohibits or inhibits human beings from actualizing the Qur'anic vision of human destiny embodied In the classic proclamation: "Towards Allah is thy limit" (Surah 53: An-Najm: 42).

Amer Haleem
"Secular and Islamic Perspective of Civil and Human Rights,"
Muslim Civil Rights Center, *www.mcrcnet.org.*

Answer: Islam rejects terrorism, and in fact considers attacks against non-combatants and innocent civilians as a major crime. The Qur'an speaks clearly: "whoever kills an innocent soul, who has not taken a life or brought destruction to society, is as if he has killed the entire humanity; and whoever saves an innocent soul is as if he has saved the entire humanity." (Al-Ma'idah 5: 32)

"*[In 2005,] the [Chinese] government's human rights record remained poor, and the government continued to commit numerous and serious abuses.*"

China Is Abusing Human Rights

U.S. State Department

In this viewpoint, the U.S. State Department lays out the human rights violations of the People's Republic of China. According to the State Department, China abuses many human rights but particularly the political and civil rights of those who are perceived to threaten the authority of the Chinese government. Harassment, torture, arbitrary arrest, and unlawful detention are serious problems in China, says the U.S. State Department. The U.S. State Department is the lead foreign affairs agency for the United States.

As you read, consider the following questions:

1. Ultimate authority in Chinese government rests with who?

2. What is the main source of organ donations in China?

U.S. State Department, "Country Reports on Human Rights Practices," *U.S. Department of State: Bureau of Democracy, Human Rights and Labor*, March 8, 2006. U.S. Department of State, Washington, DC.

3. The Chinese judiciary received policy guidance
from what two entities?

The People's Republic of China (PRC) is an authoritarian state in which, as specified in its constitution, the Chinese Communist Party (CCP) is the paramount source of power. Party members hold almost all top government, police and military positions. Ultimate authority rests with the 24-member political bureau (Politburo) of the CCP and its 9-member standing committee. General Secretary Hu Jintao holds the three most powerful positions as CCP general secretary, president, and chairman of the Central Military Commission (CMC). The party's authority rested primarily on the government's ability to maintain social stability; appeals to nationalism and patriotism; party control of personnel, media, and the security apparatus; and continued improvement in the living standards of most of the country's 1.3 billion citizens. Civilian authorities generally maintained effective control of the security forces.

Numerous Human Rights Abuses

The government's human rights record remained poor, and the government continued to commit numerous and serious abuses. There was a trend towards increased harassment, detention, and imprisonment by government and security authorities of those perceived as threatening to government authority. The government also adopted measures to control more tightly print, broadcast and electronic media, and censored online content. Protests by those seeking to redress grievances increased significantly and were suppressed, at times violently, by security forces. There were notable developments in legal reforms during the year. However, some key measures to increase the authority of the judiciary and reduce the arbitrary power of police and security forces stalled. The government adopted new religious affairs regulations expanding legal protection for some activities of registered religious groups but was criticized for failing to protect unregistered groups.

The following human rights problems were reported:

- denial of the right to change the government

- physical abuse resulting in deaths in custody

- torture and coerced confessions of prisoners

- harassment, detention, and imprisonment of those perceived as threatening to party and government authority

- arbitrary arrest and detention, including nonjudicial administrative detention, reeducation-through-labor, psychiatric detention, and extended or incommunicado pretrial detention

- a politically controlled judiciary and a lack of due process in certain cases, especially those involving dissidents

- detention of political prisoners, including those convicted of disclosing state secrets and subversion, those convicted under the now-abolished crime of counterrevolution, and those jailed in connection with the 1989 Tiananmen demonstrations

- house arrest and other nonjudicially approved surveillance and detention of dissidents

- monitoring of citizens' mail, telephone and electronic communications

- use of a coercive birth limitation policy, in some cases resulting in forced abortion and sterilization

- increased restrictions on freedom of speech and the press; closure of newspapers and journals; banning of politically sensitive books, periodicals, and films; and jamming of some broadcast signals

- restrictions on the freedom of assembly, including detention and abuse of demonstrators and petitioners

- restrictions on religious freedom, control of religious groups, and harassment and detention of unregistered religious groups

- restrictions on the freedom of travel, especially for politically sensitive and underground religious figures

- forcible repatriation of North Koreans and inadequate protection of many refugees

- severe government corruption

- increased scrutiny, harassment and restrictions on independent domestic and foreign nongovernmental organization (NGO) operations

- trafficking in women and children

- societal discrimination against women, minorities, and persons with disabilities

- cultural and religious repression of minorities in Tibetan areas and Muslim areas of Xinjiang

- restriction of labor rights, including freedom of association, the right to organize and bargain collectively, and worker health and safety

- forced labor, including prison labor

There were several positive human rights developments during the year. The government returned authority to approve death sentences to the Supreme People's Court, supported local experiments to record police interrogation of suspects, and limited the administrative detention of minors, the elderly, pregnant women, and nursing mothers. In March government officials stated that family bible studies in private homes need not be registered with the government and said that the law permitted religious education of minors, but problems continued in both areas. The National People's Congress (NPC) adopted amendments to the law protecting women's rights and interests, including one outlawing sexual harassment. The government ratified International Labor Organization (ILO) Convention 111 prohibiting discrimination in employment. The government also hosted visits by international human rights monitors. . . .

Deprivation of Life

During the year politically motivated and other arbitrary and unlawful killings occurred. While no official statistics on deaths in custody were available, state-run media reported that law enforcement officials killed 460 persons and seriously injured more than 100 through abuse or dereliction of duty in 2003. . . .

Trials involving capital offenses sometimes took place under circumstances involving severe lack of due process and with no meaningful appeal. Executions often took place on the day of conviction or failed appeal. In Xinjiang, executions of Uighurs whom authorities accused of separatism but which some observers claimed were politically motivated were reported . . . . The government regarded the number of death sentences it carried out as a state secret. However, in March 2004 an NPC deputy asserted that nearly 10 thousand cases per year "result in immediate execution," a figure Supreme People's Court (SPC) and Ministry of Justice officials stated was exaggerated. Foreign experts estimated that the country executed between 5 thousand and 12 thousand persons each year. The SPC announced its intention to take back from provincial courts the authority to approve all death sentences, an authority given to provinces during the government's 1983 anticrime "strike hard" campaign. During the year judges were hired and an administrative division established to conduct reviews of death sentences, but the SPC had not yet begun exercising its authority .... Media reports stated that approximately 10 percent of executions were for economic crimes, especially corruption. NPC officials insisted during the year that there were no plans to abolish the death penalty for economic crimes.

Disappearance

The government used incommunicado detention. The law requires notification of family members within 24 hours of detention, but individuals were often held without notification for significantly longer periods, especially in politically sensitive cases. Citizens who were reportedly detained with no or severely delayed notice included blind legal activist Chen Guangcheng, attorney Zhu Jiuhu, petitioner advocate Hou Wenzhuo, and writer Yang Maodong (also known as Guo Feixiong). In 2004 Jiang Yanyong and his wife were detained and held incommunicado for several weeks in connection with a letter he wrote to government leaders asking for reconsideration of the 1989 Tiananmen massacre....

Torture

The law forbids prison guards from extorting confessions by torture, insulting prisoners' dignity, and beating or encouraging others to beat prisoners; however, police and other elements of the security apparatus employed torture and degrading treatment in dealing with some detainees and prisoners. Officials acknowledged that torture and coerced confessions were chronic problems and began a campaign aimed at curtailing these practices. Former detainees credibly reported that officials used electric shocks, prolonged periods of solitary confinement, incommunicado detention, beatings, shackles, and other forms of abuse.

Beijing 2008

In 2008 the Olympic Games are supposed to start in Beijing. The International Olympic Committee made its decision in 2001 based on promises by Beijing bidders that the human rights situation in China would be improving. That has not clearly happened, as documented by all independent monitors.

The authoritarian government of China continues to execute more people every year than the rest of the world combined; imprison and torture people who peacefully exercise their right to freedom of expression and association; persecute Tibetan Buddhists, Uyghur Muslims, Chinese Christians and Falun Gong practitioners; deny talks about autonomy to the Tibetan people; endanger democratic processes in Taiwan and elsewhere in East Asia. Human rights are violated even in direct relation to the preparation of the Games as hundreds of thousands of Beijing residents are evicted without compensation from their homes, and those who dare to protest are often persecuted.

Joint Statement: Olympic Watch Reporters Without Borders
International Society for Human Rights Solidarité Chine Laogai
Research Foundation, August 7, 2006, www.olympicwatch.org.

After a November [2005] visit, UN Special Rapporteur on Torture Manfred Nowak concluded that torture remained widespread, although the amount and severity decreased. He reported that beatings with fists, sticks, and electric batons were the most common tortures. Cigarette burns, guard-instructed beatings by fellow inmates, and submersion in water or sewage were also reported. Nowak further found that many detainees were held for long periods in extreme positions, that death row inmates were shackled or handcuffed 24 hours per day, and that systematic abuse was designed to break the will of detainees until they confessed. Procedural and substantive measures to prevent torture were inadequate. Nowak found that members of some house church groups, Falun Gong adherents [spiritual movement banned by the PRC], Tibetans, and Uighur prisoners were specific targets of torture. The government said Nowak's preliminary report was inaccurate because he had visited only three Chinese cities (Beijing, Lhasa, and Urumqi) and urged him to revise conclusions in his final report. . . .

Prison Conditions

Conditions in penal institutions for both political prisoners and common criminals generally were harsh and frequently degrading. Prisoners and detainees often were kept in overcrowded conditions with poor sanitation. Prison capacity became an increasing problem in some areas. Food often was inadequate and of poor quality, and many detainees relied on supplemental food and medicines provided by relatives; some prominent dissidents were not allowed to receive such goods. . . .

Officials confirmed that executed prisoners were among the sources of organs for transplant. No national law governed organ donations nor were there reliable statistics on how many organ transplants using organs from executed prisoners occurred, but a Ministry of Health directive explicitly states that buying and selling human organs and tissues is not allowed. Transplant doctors stated publicly in 2003 that "the main source [of organ donations] is voluntary donations from condemned prisoners," but serious questions remained concerning whether meaningful or voluntary consent from the prisoners or their relatives was obtained.

Adequate, timely medical care for prisoners continued to be a serious problem, despite official assurances that prisoners have the right to prompt medical treatment. Labor activist Yao Fuxin suffered a heart attack in prison in August and foreign residents Yang Jianli and Wang Bingzhang previously suffered strokes in prison. In all three cases, authorities rejected their requests for outside medical care. Yao and fellow labor activist Xiao Yunliang also had to withstand frequent prison transfers while in ill health. . . .

Sexual and physical abuse and extortion were reported in some detention centers. Falun Gong activists reported that police raped female practitioners, including an incident in November at the Dongchengfang police station in Tunzhou City, Hebei Province, in which two women were raped while in detention. Forced labor in prisons and reeducation-through-labor camps was common. Juveniles were required by law to be held separately from adults, unless facilities were sufficient. In practice, children sometimes were detained without their parents, held with adults, and required to work. . . .

Arrest and Detention

Arbitrary arrest and detention remained serious problems. The law permits police and security authorities to detain persons without arresting or charging them. It also permits sentencing without trial to as many as four years in reeducation-through-labor camps and other administrative detention. Because the government tightly controlled information, it was impossible to determine accurately the total number of persons subjected to new or continued arbitrary arrest or detention. According to 2003 government statistics, more than 260 thousand persons were in reeducation-through-labor camps. Foreign experts estimated that more than 310 thousand persons were serving sentences in these camps in 2003. According to published SPP [Supreme People' Protectorate, an investigative committee] reports, the country's 340 reeducation-through-labor facilities had a total capacity of about 300 thousand persons. In addition the population of special administrative detention facilities for drug offenders and prostitutes grew rapidly following a campaign to crack down on drugs and prostitution. In 2004 these facilities held more than 350 thousand offenders, nearly three times as many as in 2002. The government also confined some Falun Gong adherents, petitioners, labor activists, and others to psychiatric hospitals.

Extended, unlawful detention remained a problem, although the government claimed to have eliminated it. In March both the SPP and the SPC told the NPC that they had resolved all cases of extended, unlawful detention. Nonetheless, a number of politically sensitive individuals were held for periods longer than that authorized by law, including journalists Zhao Yan and Ching Cheong. In some cases, investigating security agents or prosecutors sought repeated extensions, resulting in pretrial detention of a year or longer. It was uncertain how many other prisoners were similarly detained. . . .

Fair Trial

The law states that the courts shall exercise judicial power independently, without interference from administrative organs, social organizations, and individuals. However, in practice the judiciary was not independent. It received policy guidance from both the government and the CCP, whose leaders used a variety of means to direct courts on verdicts and sentences, particularly in politically sensitive cases. At both the central and local levels, the government frequently interfered in the judicial system and dictated court decisions. Trial judges decide individual cases under the direction of the trial committee in each court. In addition the CCP's law and politics committee, which include representatives of the police, security, procuratorate, and courts, had the authority to review and influence court operations at all levels of the judiciary; in some cases the committee altered decisions. Party and political leaders were known to instruct courts and judges on the handling of individual cases. People's congresses also had authority to alter court decisions, but this happened rarely. Corruption often influenced judicial decision-making and safeguards against corruption were vague and poorly enforced . . . . The people's congresses appointed judges at the corresponding level of the judicial structure. Judges received their court finances and salaries from those government bodies and could be replaced by them. This sometimes resulted in local authorities exerting undue influence over the judges they appointed and financed. . . .

Political Prisoners

Government officials continued to deny holding any political prisoners, asserting that authorities detained persons not for their political or religious views, but because they violated the law; however, the authorities continued to confine citizens for reasons related to politics and religion. Tens of thousands of political prisoners remained incarcerated, some in prisons and others in reeducation-through-labor camps and other forms of administrative detention. The government did not grant international humanitarian organizations access to political prisoners.

Western NGOs estimated that approximately 500 persons remained in prison for the repealed crime of "counterrevolution," and thousands of others were serving sentences under the state security law, which Chinese authorities stated covers crimes similar to counterrevolution. Persons detained for counterrevolutionary offenses included labor activist Hu Shigen; Inner Mongolian activist Hada; and dissidents Yu Dongyue, Zhang Jingsheng, and Sun Xiongying. Foreign governments urged the government to review the cases of those charged before 1997 with counterrevolution and to release those who had been jailed for nonviolent offenses under the old statute. During the year the government held expert-level discussions with foreign officials on conducting such a review, but no formal review was initiated. However, a number of "counterrevolutionary" prisoners were released during the year, some after receiving sentence reductions. Editor Chen Yanbin, who received a sentence reduction several years ago, was released on April 12 after spending more than 14 years in prison. The government maintained that counterrevolutionary prisoners were eligible for parole and early release on an equal basis with other non-counterrevolutionary prisoners but provided no evidence to support this assertion. . . .

Personal Freedoms

The law states that the "freedom and privacy of correspondence of citizens are protected by law"; however, the authorities often did not respect the privacy of citizens in practice. Although the law requires warrants before law enforcement officials can search premises, this provision frequently was ignored; moreover, the Public Security Bureau and the Procuratorate could issue search warrants on their own authority without judicial consent, review, or consideration. Cases of forced entry by police officers continued to be reported.

During the year authorities monitored telephone conversations, facsimile transmissions, e-mail, text messaging, and Internet communications. Authorities also opened and censored domestic and international mail. The security services routinely monitored and entered residences and offices to gain access to computers, telephones, and fax machines. All major hotels had a sizable internal security presence, and hotel guestrooms were sometimes bugged and searched for sensitive or proprietary materials.

Some citizens were under heavy surveillance and routinely had their telephone calls monitored or telephone service disrupted. The authorities frequently warned dissidents and activists, underground religious figures, former political prisoners, and others whom the government considered to be troublemakers not to meet with foreigners. During the year police ordered many such citizens not to meet with foreign journalists or diplomats, especially before sensitive anniversaries, at the time of important government or party meetings, and during the visits of high-level foreign officials. Security personnel also harassed and detained the family members of political prisoners, including following them to meetings with foreign reporters and diplomats, and urging them to remain silent about the cases of their relatives. Family members of prisoners were discouraged or prevented from meeting with the UN special rapporteur for torture. . . .

The country's birth planning policies retained harshly coercive elements in law and practice. The laws restrict the rights of families to choose the number of children they have and the period of time between births. The penalties for violating the law are strict, leaving some women little choice but to abort pregnancies. In addition implementation of the policy by local officials resulted in serious violations of human rights. Reports of forced sterilizations and abortions, in violation of the national law, continued to be documented in rural areas.

> *"The U.S. government ought to first clean up its own record of human rights before qualifying itself to comment on human rights situations in other countries, let alone arrogantly telling them what to do."*

The United States Is Abusing Human Rights

Information Office of the State Council of the People's Republic of China

In the following viewpoint, the Information Office of the State Council of the People's Republic of China (PRC) claims that the United States has violated many human rights. The PRC State Council issued this report one day after the United States State Department issued its report on the human rights abuses in China. The PRC State Council says that the United States should look at its own human rights abuses—allowing violence in America, infringing on personal freedoms, poverty and social inequality, discrimination, and the killing of innocent civilians— before it points its finger at other countries' human rights record. The State Council of the People's Republic of China is the chief administrative authority of China.

As you read, consider the following questions:

1. According to the Information Office of the People's Republic of China (PRC), how many privately owned firearms are there in the United States?
2. According to the PRC, the 2005 study by the London School of Economics found what?
3. According to the PRC, the UN High Commissioner for Human Rights, Louis Arbour, criticized the United States for doing what?

O n March 8, the U.S. Department of State, posing once again as "the world's judge of human rights," released its Country Reports on Human Rights Practices for 2005. As in previous years, the State Department pointed the finger at human rights situations in more than 190 countries and regions, including China, but kept silent on the serious violations of human rights in the United States. To help people realize the true features of this self-styled "guardian of human rights," it is necessary to probe into the human rights abuses in the United States in 2005.

Guns and Violence

For a long time, the life and personal security of people of the United States have not been under efficient protection. American society is characterized with rampant violent crimes. Across the country each year, 50,000 suicides and homicides are committed.

The U.S. Justice Department reported on Sept. 25, 2005 that there were 5,182,670 violent crimes in the United States in 2004. There were 21.4 victims for every 1,000 people aged 12 and older, which amounts to about one violent crime victim for every 47 U.S. citizens. . . .

The United States has the largest number of privately owned guns in the world. According to statistics released in June 2005 by the Brady Campaign, an organization aiming to prevent gun violence, there were approximately 192 million privately owned firearms in the United States. . . .

Democracy for the Rich

The United States has always boasted itself as the "model of democracy" and hawked its mode of democracy to the rest of the world. In fact, American "democracy" is always one for the wealthy and a "game for the rich."

The democratic elections in the United States, to a great extent, are driven by money. During the mayoral election of New York City in November 2005, billionaire Mayor Michael Bloomberg spent 77.89 million U.S. dollars of his fortune for re-election. That came to more than 100 U.S. dollars per vote. The election was termed by the *Associated Press* as the most expensive mayoral re-election in history. In the race for governor of New Jersey, the dueling multimillionaires spent 75 million U.S. dollars combined, with 40 million dollars by Jon S. Corzine, who won the election. Taking into account the 60 million U.S. dollars he spent on a Senate seat in 2000, Corzine had spent 100 million U.S. dollars in five years for elections. According to a survey, in Washington D.C. a U.S. senator needs about 20 million U.S. dollars to keep the seat in the Senate. *The Washington Post* criticized the U.S. political system in an editorial: "But a political system that turns elective office into a bauble for purchase is not a healthy one.". . .

Poverty and Social Inequality

The United States is the richest in the world, but its poverty rate is also the highest among the developed countries. In the United States, problems such as poverty, hunger and homelessness are quite serious, and the economic, social and cultural rights of working people are not guaranteed.

A study of eight advanced countries by London School of Economics in 2005 found that the United States had the worst social inequality, Reuters reported on April 25, 2005. The poverty rate of the United States is the highest in the developed world and more than twice as high as in most other industrialized countries. In recent years the fortunes of the rich have continued to rise in the United States. According to two new studies by Spectrem Group, a Chicago-based wealth-research firm, and the Boston Consulting Group, millionaire households (excluding the value of primary residences) in the United States controlled more than 11 trillion dollars in assets in 2004, up more than 8 percent from 2003. Meanwhile, the income of ordinary employees in the United States has seen a sharp decline, causing the increase of poor population. The data issued by the U.S. Census Bureau said that the nation's official poverty rate rose from 12.5 percent in 2003 to 12.7 percent in 2004, with the number of people in poverty rising by 1.1 million from 35.9 million to 37 million, which means one in eight Americans lived in poverty. Poverty rates in cities such as Detroit, Miami and Newark exceeded 28 percent. The *New York Times* reported on Nov 22, 2005 that in 2004 3.9 million families had members who were undernourished. . . .

Personal Freedoms

There exist serious infringements upon personal rights and freedoms by law enforcement and judicial organs in the United States.

Secret snooping is prevalent and illegal detention occurs from time to time. The recently disclosed Snoopgate scandal has aroused keen attention of the public in the United States. After the Sept. 11, 2001 terrorist attacks, the U.S. President has for dozens of times authorized the National Security Agency and other departments to wiretap some domestic phone calls. With this authorization, the National Security Agency may conduct surveillance over phone calls and e-mails of 500 U.S. citizens at a time. It is reported that from 2002 through 2004, there were at least 287 cases in which special agents of FBI were suspected of illegally conducting electronic surveillance.

U.N. Investigating U.S. Human Rights Abuses

The U.N. Human Rights Committee, scheduled to meet in Geneva in October 2005, has written to non-governmental organizations (NGOs) calling for any available evidence of human rights abuses by the United States—particularly in the aftermath of its global war on terrorism.

The 18-member committee, comprised of independent human rights experts, will take up "issues of specific concerns relating to the effect of measures taken (by the administration of President George W. Bush) in the fight against terrorism following the events of 11 September 2001," the day the United States was subject to terrorist attacks.

The primary focus will be "on the implications of the USA Patriot Act on nationals and non-nationals, as well as problems relating to the legal status and treatment of persons detained in Afghanistan, Guantanamo, Iraq and other places of detention outside the USA."

Thalif Deen,
"UN Human Rights Body to Scrutinize U.S. Abuses,"
Common Dreams News Center Inter Press Service,
September 21, 2005.

In one of the cases, an FBI agent conducted secret surveillance of an American citizen for five years without notifying the U.S. Department of Justice. On Dec. 21, 2005, the U.S. Senate voted to extend the Patriot Act, a move that aroused keen concern of public opinion. The law makes it easier for FBI agents to monitor phone calls and e-mails, to search homes and offices, and to obtain the business records of terrorism suspects. According to a report of the U.S. National Broadcasting Company on Dec. 13, 2005, the U.S. Defense Department had been secretly collecting information about U.S. citizens opposing the Iraq war and secretly monitoring all meetings for peace and against the war. According to a report of the *New York Times*, in recent years, FBI had been collecting information on large numbers of non-governmental organizations that participated in anti-war demonstrations everywhere in the United States through its monitoring network and other channels. The volume of collected information is stunning. Among it, there are 2,400 pages of information on Greenpeace, an environmental group. On Jan. 9, 2006, a spokeswoman for the U.S. Bureau of Customs and Border Protection announced that in the "anti-terrorism" fight the U.S. customs has the right to open and inspect incoming private letters, which again sparked protests. On Jan. 17, 2006, the American Civil Liberties Union and the New York-based Center for Constitutional Rights separately filed suits in U.S. district court for eastern Michigan and a federal court against the U.S. President and heads of security agencies for spying on U.S. citizens. . . .

Racial Discrimination

The United States is a multi-ethnic nation of immigrants, with minority ethnic groups accounting for more than one-fourth of its population. But racial discrimination has long been a chronic malady of American society. Black Americans and other ethnic minorities are at the bottom of American society and their living standards are much lower than that of whites. According to *The State of Black America 2005*, the income level of African American families is only one-tenth of that of white families, and the welfare enjoyed by black Americans is only three-fourths of their white counterparts. In 2004, the poverty rate was 24.7 percent for African Americans, 21.9 percent for Hispanics, and 8.6 percent for non-Hispanic whites. In New Orleans, 100,000 of its 500,000 population live in poverty, with the majority of them being black Americans.

The homeownership rate for blacks is 48.1 percent compared with 75.4 percent for whites. *The Washington Post* reported on April 11, 2005 that in 2004, about 29 percent of African Americans who bought or refinanced homes ended up with high-cost loans, compared with only about 10 percent of white Americans. . . .

Gender Discrimination

The United States does not have a good record in safeguarding the rights of women and children.

Women in the United States do not share equal rights and opportunities with men in politics. Despite the fact that women account for 51.1 percent of the U.S. population, they hold only 81 or 15.1 percent of the 535 seats in the 109th U.S. Congress, including 14 or 14 percent of the 100 Senate seats and 67 or 15.4 percent of the 435 seats in the House of Representatives. Only eight (16 percent) of the governors of 50 U.S. states are women. No women of color have ever been governor of a U.S. state. Just 14 of the mayors of America's largest 100 cities are women, accounting for 14 percent of the total. By November 2005, there were only 81 women serving in statewide executive office, 25.7 percent of the total 315 working posts. Of the 7,382 people serving in the state legislatures, 1,668 are women, accounting for 22.6 percent. A research by the Inter-Parliamentary Union showed the United States ranked 61st in terms of women's representation in national legislature or parliaments out of over 180 directly electing countries, down from the 58th in December 2003. . . .

Innocent Civilians Killed

Pursuing unilateralism on the international arena, the U.S. government grossly violates the sovereignty and human rights of other countries in contempt of universally-recognized international norms.

The U.S. government frequently commits wanton slaughters of innocents in its war efforts and military operations in other countries. *The USA Today* newspaper on Dec. 13, 2005 quoted a 2004 study published in the medical journal *The Lancet* as saying that it was estimated that about 100,000 Iraqis, mostly women and children, had died in the Iraqi war launched by the U.S. government in 2003. The year 2005 also witnessed frequent overseas military operations targeted at civilians by the U.S. forces, causing quite a number of deaths and injuries. On July 4, 2005, the U.S. forces killed 17 civilians, including women and children, in their air strikes in Konarha Province of Afghanistan. On Aug. 12, a U.S. military armored patrol vehicle fired at people coming out of a mosque in a town in the suburbs of the Iraqi city of Ramdi, killing 15 Iraqis, including eight children, and injuring 17 others. On Aug. 30, U.S. jet fighters launched several sorties of air raids against an area near the western Iraqi border town of Qaim, causing at least 56 deaths, including elderlies and children. On Nov. 21, U.S. troops fired at a civilian vehicle in northern Baghdad, killing a family of five, including three children. On Jan. 14, 2006, U.S. military aircraft struck a Pakistani village bordering Afghanistan, killing at least 18 civilians and triggering widespread anti-U.S. demonstrations in Pakistan. . . .

The U.S. government's violations of internationally recognized norms and human rights incurred strong international condemnation. At a press conference, the UN High Commissioner for Human Rights Louis Arbour sharply criticized the United States for infringing human rights by setting up secret prisons and transferring terrorism suspects without going through legal procedures under the pretext of fighting terrorism, noting that such acts were eroding the global ban on torture. On Dec. 20, 2005, the European Union, through a local court in Milan, Italy, issued warrants for the arrest of 22 CIA agents suspected of kidnapping in Italy. Former U.S. President Jimmy Carter described the prisoner abuse by the U.S. military in Iraq, Afghanistan and Guantanamo as "embarrassing," and going against the rudimentary American commitment to peace, social justice, civil liberties and human rights.

The United States Is Hypocritical

The facts listed above show a poor human rights record of the United States, which forms not only a sharp contrast with its image of a self-claimed "advocate of human rights," but also disaccord with its level of economic and social development and international status. The U.S. government ought to first clean up its own record of human rights before qualifying itself to comment on human rights situations in other countries, let alone arrogantly telling them what to do.

To respect for and protect human rights is a necessity and indicator of human civilization, and to promote human rights is the common responsibility of all countries and a major theme of international cooperation. No country in the world can claim to have a perfect state of human rights, nor can any country stay outside the course of human rights development. The issue of human rights should become a theme of social development in all countries and of international cooperation, rather than a slogan for exporting ideologies or even a tool of diplomacy to fix others out of one's own political needs.

For years, the U.S. government has ignored and deliberately concealed serious violations of human rights in its own country for fear of criticism. Yet it has issued annual reports making unwarranted charges on human rights practices of other countries, an act that fully exposes its hypocrisy and double standard on human rights issues, which has naturally met with strong resistance and opposition from other countries. We urge the U.S. government to look squarely at its own human rights problems, reflect what it has done in the human rights field and take concrete measures to improve its own human rights status. The U.S. government should stop provoking international confrontation on the issue of human rights, and make a fresh start to contribute more to interna-

tional human rights cooperation and to the healthy development of international human rights cause.

Periodical Bibliography

The following articles have been selected to supplement the diverse views presented in this chapter.

Omar al Bashir — "Sudan: 'We're All Africans, We're All Black,'" *New African*, April 2007.

Jennifer Chou — "Out for Justice; Chinese Lawyers Are Opening a New Front in the Nation's Struggle for Human Rights," *Weekly Standard*, August 24, 2006.

Patricia Esquenazi — "A Day of Dawning Peace in Haiti," *Americas*, May–June 2006.

Anthony Fenton — "Legalized Imperialism: 'Responsibility to Protect' and the Dubious Case of Haiti," *Briarpatch*, December 2005.

Pallovi Gogoi — "Wal-Mart's Record on Human Rights; A Report From Human Rights Watch Accuses the Retailing Giant of Going to Extreme Lengths to Prevent Workers From Forming Unions," *Business Week Online*, May 2, 2007.

Lindsey Hilsum — "Yes, We Have No Political Prisoners (China)," *New Statesman*, December 11, 2006.

Rosalyn Karugonjo — "Continent Riddled by Human Rights Violations," *The Monitor*, May 16, 2007.

Craig and Marc Kielburger — "Love Hurts When Wars Paid for By Gem Trade," *Toronto Star*, February 15, 2007.

Roland Bankole Marke — "No Compassion for Sierra Leone's Amputees," *Worldpress.org*, March 29, 2007.

Physicians for Human Rights — "Epidemic of Inequality: Women's Rights and HIV/AIDS in Botswana & Swaziland," Physicians for Human Rights, 2007.

UN General Assembly — "Putting People First in Development; Third Committee: Social, Humanitarian and Cultural," *UN Chronicle*, March–May, 2005.

CHAPTER 3

What Should Be Done to Stop Human Rights Abuses?

Chapter Preface

The Nobel Peace Prize is the name of one of five Nobel Prizes bequeathed by the Swedish industrialist and inventor Alfred Nobel. When Nobel died in 1896 he left a vast estate. His will stated that he wished his estate to be turned into a fund and the interest gained on the fund would be used to award annual prizes to those who, "during the preceding year shall have conferred the greatest benefit on mankind." Nobel had declared that the interest should be divided into five equal parts and distributed to those making the most important discoveries to advance mankind in the fields of physics, chemistry, physiology or medicine, literature, and peace. According to Nobel, the peace prize should go to "the person who shall have done the most or the best work for fraternity between nations, for the abolition or reduction of standing armies and for the holding and promotion of peace congresses." Exploring the Nobel Peace Prize and its winners over the years provides a glimpse into the history of those who have fought to protect human rights.

The first Nobel Peace Prize, awarded in 1901, was shared by Frenchman Frédéric Passy founder and president of the first French peace society (Société d'arbitrage entre les Nations) and Swiss humanitarian Jean Henri Dunant, founder of the Red Cross and originator of the Geneva Conventions. In addition to Dunant receiving the Peace Prize for founding the Red Cross, the organization itself received the prize three different times. In 1917 and 1944, the International Committee for the Red Cross (ICRC), was honored with the only Peace prizes awarded during the times of World War I (1914–1918) and World War II (1939–1944) because it "held aloft the fundamental conceptions of the solidarity of the human race." The ICRC's third Peace Prize was granted in 1963, marking the 100th anniversary of Dunant's founding of the organization.

In 1977, the Nobel Peace Prize was also shared. The prize was given to the organization Amnesty International and the initiators of the Northern Ireland Peace Movement. Upon announcing the prizes, Aase Lionæs, Chairman of the Norwegian Nobel Committee, said "These two movements have one thing in common: they have sprung spontaneously from the individual's deep and firmly rooted conviction that the ordinary man and woman is capable of making a meaningful contribution to peace. The two prizewinners have given a clear and simple No to violence, torture, and terrorism, and an equally clear and unreserved Yes to the defence of human dignity and human rights."

Jody Williams and the International Campaign to Ban Landmines (ICBL) were honored with the Peace Prize in 1997 for their work to eradicate land mines. According to the United Nations Mine Action Service, land mines and explosive remnants of war indiscriminately kill or maim thousands of people every year and children are frequent victims. In 1997, it was estimated that there were probably over one hundred million antipersonnel mines scattered over large areas on several continents. However, due to the work of Jody Williams and the ICBL, significant progress has been made to reduce the numbers of land mines throughout the world. Williams and the ICBL strive to find and destroy land mines, to get countries to stop making and using land mines, and to help the victims of land mine explosions.

The list of Nobel Peace Prize laureates includes many human rights advocates, including Martin Luther King Jr. (1964); Mother Teresa (1979); Aung San Suu Kyi (1991); Kofi Annan (2001); former U.S. President Jimmy Carter (2002); and former U.S. Vice President Al Gore (2007).

Each year as the Nobel Peace Prize is awarded it reminds us that the world is still not free of war, atrocities, and human rights abuses. However, it also reminds us that there are individuals and organizations from all over the globe willing to fight against human rights abuses. Additionally, the diversity of people and organizations receiving the Nobel Peace Prize illustrates that there are a multitude of ways to promote human rights and to prevent human rights abuses. The authors in the following chapter discuss what they think should be done to stop human rights abuses.

> "Obviously the United Nations is not a
> perfect organization, but it is a neces-
> sary one."

The United Nations Is Necessary to Stop Human Rights Abuses

Silvano Tomasi

In this viewpoint, Silvano Tomasi writes that although the United Nations needs reform, the organization is still needed to defend and promote human rights in the twenty-firstst century. Tomasi says the world needs an organization that is centered on the fundamental rights of "persons," not national interests, cultures, or religions. A reformed human rights–based United Nations can govern the international community in the 21st century, says Tomasi. Archbishop Silvano Tomasi is the Catholic Church's permanent observer to the United Nations at Geneva.

As you read, consider the following questions:

1. What three documents does Tomasi refer to as the juridical architecture that the twentieth century left behind as its heritage for the future?

Silvano M. Tomasi, "United Nations Reform and Human Rights," *America*, vol. 193, September 12, 2005, Copyright 2005, www.americamagazine.org. All rights reserved. Reproduced by permission of America Press. For subscription information, visit www.americamagazine.org.

2. The war on poverty and the phenomenon of terrorism both find what in human rights, states Tomasi? Explain.

3. According to the author, what are the major criticisms of the Commission on Human Rights?

The world is busy debating the reform of the United Nations [U.N.]. In mid-September [of 2005] a rendezvous with history is anticipated in New York City: a summit of heads of states and governments to decide up-to-date structures for the governance of the planet. In 1945, in the aftermath of a bloody and destructive war of unprecedented cruelty, 51 countries, led by the winner nations, decided to launch a project, both ambitious and tough, to protect peace in the world. Sixty years later, 191 countries still struggle to achieve the goals set out in the first lines of the United Nations Charter: to prevent the scourge of war; to reaffirm faith in the fundamental human rights, in the dignity and worth of the human person, in the equal rights of men and women and of nations large and small; to respect, treaties; and to promote progress and freedom.

United Nations Is Necessary

These noble goals remain guidelines for the governance of the international community, as world leaders meet at the Millennium Summit this month. They have been formulated in the context of an impressive juridical architecture that the 20th century left behind as its heritage for the future: the Charter of the United Nations, the Universal Declaration on Human Rights and the four Geneva Conventions of 1949. For half a century, the reality on the ground was marked by a cold war, more than 100 regional hot wars and several genocides. Then the new century ushered in a novelty in the strategic use of violence: terrorism with suicide bombers, with nonstate actors using war tactics and attacks on civilians, and provoking equally nontraditional forms of response. At its beginning, the

Sixtieth Anniversary United Nations General Assembly

Throughout the last 60 years, the Assembly has taken landmark decisions on matters in which all humanity has an interest—from the Universal Declaration of Human Rights in 1948 to the Millennium Development Goals in 2000. And the United Nations has overseen an enormous amount of practical activity to promote development, democracy and human rights; protect the environment; and maintain peace and security.

Now, the Assembly has responsibilities encompassing both old and new threats and challenges in the fields of international security, development and poverty reduction, communicable diseases, human rights, humanitarian assistance, non-proliferation and disarmament, and counterterrorism.

But some defining characteristics have not changed. The General Assembly remains the world's single universal intergovernmental body. And in September 2005, the largest-ever gathering of world leaders reaffirmed "the central role of the General Assembly as the chief deliberative, policymaking and representative organ of the United Nations".

The words of Dr. Zuleta Angel of Colombia, the opening speaker on 10 January 1946, are strikingly relevant today. He said:

"The whole world now awaits our decisions, and rightly—yet with understandable anxiety—looks to us now to show ourselves capable of mastering our problems."

Jan Eliasson, General Assembly President on Occasion of the Sixtieth Anniversary of United Nations General Assembly, January 10, 2006, U.N. GA GA/sm/366 GA/10445.

21st century shows also a persistent gap between rich and poor countries, with the entire African continent further marginalized, and the H.I.V./AIDS pandemic killing some 8,000 people a day.

Questions about the usefulness of the United Nations declarations and agreements seem a logical first step. If the right to life is denied, civil and political liberties ignored and the right to development forgotten, then the temptation follows to look at the United Nations as an old, rusty machine weighed down by a nontransparent bureaucracy or as a supranational authority often distant from the feelings of ordinary people and quite different from the organization meant to serve national governments in specific sectors of their activity.

Obviously the United Nations is not a perfect organization, but it is a necessary one. Good Pope John XXIII had already written in his encyclical Peace on Earth (1963): no state can adequately pursue its own interests in isolation from the rest nor develop as it should. The prosperity and progress of any state is in part consequence and in part cause of the prosperity and progress of all other states. The pope saw the observance of all the rights and freedoms linked to the personal dignity of every human being as the way forward. He wished therefore that the United Nations "may be able progressively to adapt its structure and methods of operation to the magnitude and nobility of its tasks."

Many Proposals to Reform the U.N.

Now all players have placed their cards on the table of reform. The High-Level Panel on Threats, Challenges and Change, created by U.N. Secretary General Kofi Annan has published its report, A More Secure World: Our Shared Responsibility. In anticipation of the review of the 2000 Millennium Declaration, the secretary general has presented his report, *In Larger Freedom: Towards Development, Security and Human Rights for All*. The U.N. high commissioner for human rights has issued

The OHCHR [Office of the United Nations High Commissioner for Human Rights] Plan of Action: Protection and Empowerment. States and nongovernmental organizations have taken public positions on the global reform of the United Nations or on changes in specific agencies. In all this flurry of proposals, particular political visibility has been given to the Security Council and its possible enlargement.

But the theme of human rights and the needed institutional framework to defend and promote them have also attracted much attention. In fact, it is becoming clearer that peace and development cannot be sustained unless rooted in human rights. Without a guarantee of the dignity of the human person, issues of security, terrorism, freedom of religion and belief, poverty, the environment and similar themes of primary importance cannot be properly and effectively dealt with. Human rights become the touchstone to measure the soundness of international relations and of the political and legal systems of states.

Examples from the international agenda of the Commission on Human Rights support this understanding. The war on poverty, in its diverse forms and strategies, and the phenomenon of terrorism, in its causes and activities of prevention and repression, both find in human rights a precise framework. Such a framework is made up of ethical values, of principles and judicial norms directed at regulating the behavior of states, the functioning of intergovernmental institutions, and providing space for the contribution of nongovernmental organizations and civil society.

We Should Renew the U.N. and Focus on Human Rights

Against this background, a renewal of the United Nations based on human rights is critical. Mechanisms and procedures for the protection of human rights should take central stage. The 53-country U.N. Commission on Human Rights is under the spotlight. Secretary General Kofi Annan proposes a remarkable change to transform it into a council that would meet more frequently, with a larger regular budget to strengthen its independence, and with provisions that would block egregious transgressors of human rights from being elected to this council. Human rights, along with security and development, are one of the three pillars of the United Nations. There is a general desire that the new council should have a higher rank, either as a subsidiary body of the General Assembly—and not, as it is now, of the Economic and Social Council—or as a council parallel to the Security Council and ECOSOC.

The United Nations Charter (Art. 1, 3) placed human rights among the essential purposes of the organization. A coherent reform would make sure that human rights not only have visibility and priority, but that they also permeate the whole structure of the U.N. system. When, for example, the Security Council envisions the use of force in the most destabilizing situations, a concerted definition for exercising the responsibility to protect human rights, particularly of the innocent, should be reached with the proposed Council on Human Rights. A similar convergence and collaboration should be foreseen with the projected Peace-Building Commission. In addition, credibility for the new body for human rights demands that, while always upholding the universality of human rights it avoid being an elitist club reserved to a small group of states without the inclusion of regional and cultural sensibilities.

Focus on the Person

Major criticisms of the Commission on Human Rights have been its politicization and the glaring deficit of implementation of the decisions reached. Will the change of name remedy the evident shortcomings? Perhaps a deeper reflection is in order at this moment of transition. The foundation of human rights is at times blurred by cultural differences, religious views, economic theories and behavioral models. In the U.N. context, a pragmatic and utilitarian approach takes hold in the analysis and evaluation of situations, in the interpretations of existing juridical instruments where the human person as such, in his or her physical, social and spiritual dimension, is replaced by sets of categories with parallel fragmented rights. In this way, rights are related to specific interests and no longer to the common good. The meeting point where different intellectual traditions can converge and where the universality of fundamental human rights can be sustained is the human person and the person's inalienable dignity, a dignity that does not change in relation to geographical coordinates or historical events. A lasting and effective reform cannot move away from this center of gravity that is the human person without losing its bearing and risking a juridical relativism that dangerously fluctuates with the changes of majority opinion.

Many insist that Special Procedures, the group of experts of the Sub-Commission on Promotion and Protection of Human Rights, and the Treaty Bodies will find their appropriate space in the reformed human rights structure. Indeed these subsidiary organs have provided an important advisory and monitoring service. When, however, they move away from the centrality of the person as the source of rights, they then introduce interpretations that in their pragmatic intent, to meet particular interests, do not take into account the concrete consequences in the long run for the common good.

Looking ahead, the reform proposes a new council, a stronger Office of the Commissioner for Human Rights, a greater role for the organs of control established by the conventions regarding human rights (Treaty Bodies) and more money for the training of experts and functionaries. The unified procedures for the Treaty Bodies will tend to transform them into a unified system of control on the activity of states in the area of human rights and into a court of judgment.

A Common Human Future

The overall reform of the United Nations aims explicitly at making the protection of human rights a key element of international governance, a synergy among persons, people, governments, civil society and international organizations, capable of intervening in critical areas for the future of the human family: peaceful solution of conflicts, prevention of wars, socio-economic cooperation and sustainability of the environment. A coherent application of the principle of subsidiarity will make it possible to reach these objectives. Suggestions and ideas have to start from below, from a well-informed public opinion capable of formulating its proposals with credibility.

The United Nations reform hopes to lead the organization back to its founding ideals and make it the center of coordination of the activity of the nations of the world. The road to achieve the dream is that of human rights. The balance of power and force among states, alone, will stall the process; but keeping the human person, human dignity and human rights will provide an opening for human flourishing in our common global future.

> *"The UN's corruption can be traced to the 1940s, when it first took up the issue of human rights."*

The United Nations Is Ineffective and Corrupt and Does Not Stop Human Rights Abuses

Joseph Loconte

In this viewpoint, Joseph Loconte claims the United Nations (UN) has been sabotaged by repressive governments and is not effective in stopping human rights abuses. Loconte says the United Nations was corrupted from its very beginning when social and economic goals were given equal status with human rights. Loconte proposes a U.S.-based alternative to the UN that functions along with other national groups and has strong input from the American evangelical community. Joseph Loconte is a senior fellow at the Ethics and Public Policy Center, an organization that strives to link domestic and foreign policy issues to the Judeo-Christian moral tradition.

Joseph Loconte, "The United Nations' Disarray: The Decline of the Human-Rights Agenda, and What Evangelicals Can Do About It," *Christianity Today*, vol. 51, February 2007. Reproduced by permission of the author.

As you read, consider the following questions:

1. According to Loconte, what was the "original sin" of the Universal Declaration of Human Rights?

2. According to Loconte, "utopianism" has nurtured what? What is utopianism according to Loconte?

3. Who does *New York Times* columnist Nicholas Kristof call the "new internationalists?"

Not long ago, I joined a Washington luncheon with Shashi Tharoor, an undersecretary general at the United Nations [UN]. Tharoor, a candidate to replace Kofi Annan [in 2006] as head of the UN, speaks with the polish and assurance of the quintessential UN diplomat. But when asked why repressive states such as China and Saudi Arabia should be allowed to serve on the UN's premier human-rights body, he hesitated. "You don't advance human rights," Tharoor insisted, "by preaching only to the converted."

Here on display is the flawed idealism of the UN's human-rights agenda, as if having human-rights abusers judging human-rights cases is the way to convert them. It is the same utopian impulse that lies behind multilateralism (the idea that nations should always act in concert) and its cousin multiculturalism (openness to the traditions and values of other cultures) and causes such confusion about human rights. Though helpful in some contexts, these ideas are slavishly applied in international politics in ways that assault the concepts of natural rights and moral norms enshrined not only in our Declaration of Independence, but also in the UN's Universal Declaration of Human Rights.

The unconverted states, of course, have hijacked human-rights ideals for their own despotic purposes. A 2004 UN task force report lamented a "legitimacy deficit" in the organization's commitment to human rights. A year later, Kofi Annan admitted that the United Nations was "passing through the gravest crisis of its existence" because of its tarnished record. He finally recommended that the Human Rights Commission be abolished and replaced by a reconstituted Human Rights Council, an idea approved by the General Assembly last year. It appears, however, that the Human Rights Council already shares in the foibles of its discredited predecessor.

In the midst of the UN's moral havoc, evangelicals—because of our theological and political commitment to human rights, especially religious freedom—have a unique and important role to play.

Bad Beginnings: Human Rights Confused with Social and Economic Goals

The UN's corruption can be traced to the 1940s, when it first took up the issue of human rights. The original Human Rights Commission, chaired by Eleanor Roosevelt, drafted a Universal Declaration of Human Rights (1948), now considered the Magna Carta of the modern human-rights movement. The original sin of that document, however, was that it confused "inalienable" human rights with social and economic aspirations. The Western idea of rights as moral claims against the coercive power of the state was put on the same footing as social benefits and government entitlements. Thus, the Universal Declaration ranks the right to "periodic holidays with pay" (Article 24) no differently than the right to life, freedom from slavery, and freedom of religion (Articles 3, 4, and 18).

No wonder people such as Charles Malik, the Lebanese delegate to the commission, were so troubled by the result. Speaking in 1952, just four years later, he warned that "a quiet revolution" had overtaken its work. "The archetype of what we were trying to ensure was freedom from discrimination and from arbitrary arrest, and freedom of religion and speech. It never occurred to us that anything else was as important as these were," Malik said. "Today, the emphasis has shifted. Economic, social, and cultural rights have come into their own." He went on to call this "the materialistic revolution of the times."

Every materialistic revolution in modern times—socialism, communism, fascism—has held a utopian vision. By definition, utopians deny the deep sinfulness of human nature. At the same time, they lose sight of the sacred basis for human dignity, the imago Dei. The result is a confusion (and ultimately a denial) of inalienable human rights. The UN version of this revolution is no different: Its multicultural creed has produced a torrent of treaties and conventions, with ever-expanding categories of rights. Nations even claim an "inalienable right" to nuclear technology (see the Nuclear Non-Proliferation Treaty, Article IV). When human rights are confused with social or economic goals, human dignity is debased—and basic rights become more politically tenuous.

Hug-a-Thug Mentality: Repressive Governments Allowed In

This helps explain why the UN General Assembly, five years after the attacks of 9/11, lacks the moral clarity to even agree on a definition of terrorism. It is why the Security Council, despite its lofty rhetoric, cannot rise above narrow political interests to stop the genocidal violence in Sudan. Finally, this utopianism has nurtured a human-rights regime that rewards the world's most repressive governments with membership and voting privileges.

Of the 53 member states of the old Human Rights Commission, for example, at least 25 percent were considered "not free" by leading human-rights organizations. (At the nadir of its corruption, the commission nominated Libya as its chair and re-elected Sudan amid reports of ethnic cleansing.) During the last two decades, attempts to produce resolutions critical of human-rights violators routinely died in their crib—blocked in backroom maneuvers.

It's doubtful that any of this will change under the new regime. The General Assembly failed to set any criteria for membership in the Human Rights Council. Governments need only a simple majority of General Assembly votes to join. Thus, the proportion of autocratic states in the body (scaled down to 47 members) remains about the same. Iran did not make the cut, but China, Cuba, Russia, and Saudi Arabia easily pocketed enough votes. The Islamic Conference, with 56 nations, can effectively block United States admission.

Moreover, the council appears to have the same hug-a-thug mentality: At the conclusion of its first and second meetings [in 2006], members failed to produce a resolution on behalf of the victims in Sudan and singled out only one country among 192 UN member states for special criticism: Israel. "Most of the world's abuses were ignored," reported UN Watch, the Geneva-based human-rights group. Peggy Hicks, global advocacy director of Human Rights Watch, agreed: "In the face of atrocities in Sudan, attacks on civilians in Sri Lanka, and impunity for mass murder in Uzbekistan, this council was largely silent."

Unfortunately, this moral chauvinism is not limited to the UN bureaucracy and its affiliates. Two years ago, for example, Amnesty International noisily condemned the U.S. war on terror as "the most sustained attack on human rights and international law in 50 years." To be sure, the abuse of prisoners at Abu Ghraib (the catalyst for Amnesty's condemnation) is a despicable episode in U.S. foreign policy. But think of it: There was no mention of the atrocities under Stalin, Mao, Pol Pot, or Saddam Hussein. No reference to the killing fields of Darfur, the child soldiers of Africa, the women sold into sexual slavery in Eastern Europe, or the hundreds of thousands of dissidents languishing in Chinese prisons.

Religious progressives echo the partisan cant of their secular counterparts. Just as the humanitarian crisis in Darfur hit a fever pitch, the World Council of Churches lambasted the

U.N. Has Failed Miserably

The United Nations began with a bang. Well, two big bangs. The two atomic bombs dropped on Japan in August of 1945 signified a beginning to a new world order of peace. Or, at least, an attempt at it. The League of Nations had already failed years earlier due to internal squabbling and legal bottlenecks. This was the opportunity for a new beginning and the possibility of one united planet, whose common goal was to promote peaceful coexistence.

As of today, this whole dream has faded into the wind, and failed miserably. As of today, the United Nations is nothing more than a combination of the League of Nations and a corrupt, for-profit charity organization. Granted, in the past, the United Nations has, as a whole, provided relief to certain countries in need. There are still many other countries that are on their proverbial "to-do" list, and others which have been flat out ignored. The past and present actions of the United Nations detail a laundry list of fraud, dishonesty, and devious practices.

James Mack Jr., "United Nations Corrupt, Uncooperative, Ineffective," The Triangle, *October 8, 2004, www.thetriangle.org.*

United States in its "Decade to Overcome Violence." The *Christian Century* ran articles calling for a "season of repentance" for U.S. actions in Iraq and elsewhere. No other nation, it seemed, had anything to repent of. A 2005 study by the Institute on Religion and Democracy found that of 197 human-rights criticisms by mainline churches from 2000 to 2003, nearly 70 percent ware aimed at America and Israel—but none at China, Libya, Syria, or North Korea. Few at the UN spoke up last year [2006] when Venezuelan dictator Hugo Chavez called George W. Bush the devil.

"Clean Hands" Charge A Ploy to Divert Attention

Why this selective indignation? Because many human-rights groups and denominational elites are heavily invested in the UN as a "parliament of humanity." They kept quiet last year, for example, as foreign ambassadors blasted the United States for its plan to reform the Human Rights Commission. UN apologists were shocked—yes, shocked—at the proposition that states under UN sanction for human-rights abuses be kept off the new Human Rights Council. Ijaz Hussein, a Pakistani educator and political analyst, captured the mood perfectly: "There is a general feeling that the U.S. is hypocritical," he wrote, "because whereas it fulminates against the election of human-rights abusers, its own hands are not clean."

The "clean hands" charge is repeated everywhere nowadays—as a ploy to divert attention from thuggish regimes. We've heard the argument before. Apologists and appeasers of the 1930s used it to divert attention from Nazi brutalities. To many progressives, Britain and the United States were equally to blame, as corrupt democracies driven by craven economic interests.

Protestant thinkers such as Reinhold Niebuhr knew better. A leading American critic of Hitler's Germany, Niebuhr called it "sheer moral perversity" to equate the failings of democratic states with the atrocities of fascist dictatorships. The "clean hands" argument, he said, was a sop to evade political responsibility. "As if any one ever came to any significant issue in history with 'clean hands'! As if any nation which enforces peace within its boundaries had clean hands!" he wrote. The "simple moralism" of the equivocators, Niebuhr argued, was a symptom of their "utopian illusions" about social and political life.

Then and now, false hopes about human nature and human societies fail to advance the cause of human rights. Under the new rules for the Human Rights Council, for example, not even genocidal regimes may be categorically denied membership. The editorial page of The *New York Times* called the latest UN plan a "shameful charade" that will not change the corrupted status quo. "John Bolton is right; Secretary General Kofi Annan is wrong," announced *The Times*. "And leading international human rights groups have unwisely put their preference for multilateral consensus ahead of their duty to fight for the strongest possible human rights protection."

Charles Malik, who assumed leadership of the old Human Rights Commission after [first lady] Eleanor Roosevelt, anticipated this result. An Arab Christian and political philosopher, Malik saw a spiritual problem at work: the rejection of belief in God and love for God as the surest foundation for defending those made in his image. Malik said that human beings possessed moral and spiritual capacities that deserved unique political safeguards—a direct challenge to Marxist materialism. "Unless man's proper nature, unless his mind and spirit are brought out, set apart, protected, and promoted, the struggle for human rights is a sham and a mockery."

We need a different kind of revolution in human-rights thinking. Neither the utopians nor the cynics are up to the task. We need a heavy dose of realism—not realpolitik, but the Christian realism of statesmen and religious leaders who anchor human rights in a transcendent view of the human person.

Evangelical Engagement

What might this mean in terms of engagement by evangelicals, whom *The New York Times* columnist Nicholas Kristof calls "the new internationalists"? First, we must help redefine human rights for the broader political community. We can remind decision makers that democratic rights owe a great debt to the Judeo-Christian conception of human dignity. We can explain why the fundamental rights of life, liberty, and freedom of worship are essential to our God-given nature.

Second, evangelical leaders and activists should endorse the idea of an alliance of democracies to work inside and outside the UN system to advance this vision of human rights. Congress has already approved a Democracy Caucus, to function as a voting bloc within the United Nations. But the organization has failed to push aggressively for democratic reforms. Evangelicals, mobilized around several key human-rights issues, could help catalyze the Democracy Caucus into effective action.

An American Alternative to the UN

Third, evangelicals could lobby for the creation of a U.S. Commission on Human Rights, in the same way they rallied in the 1990s for a U.S. Commission on International Religious Freedom. A U.S. Commission on Human Rights would not function alone, however, but would join with other national groups to offer an alternative to the United Nations. It would focus on the world's most serious rights violations: state-sanctioned torture, sexual slavery, ethnic cleansing, and genocide.

If we hope to advance the cause of human rights, we need to recover their moral and spiritual bedrock. We must work, philosophically and politically, to reconnect human dignity to a biblical view of the human person. "There is already in the great American tradition," Malik said, "grounded in Christian freedom and charity and in faith in the infinite worth of the individual human soul, the necessary elements for a satisfactory solution."

The American tradition of which Malik spoke has taken a beating in world opinion. Cynicism about our commitment to human rights is widespread. Nevertheless, by any rational measure, the American vision remains the most powerful force for human rights and democratic freedom in the world today. Still, there remains much work to be done in the task of reform and renewal, once again rooted in Christian freedom and Christian charity.

For those whose human rights hang daily in the balance—in prisons, refugee camps, and, the world's war zones—the sooner more of us begin this noble work of faith, the better.

> *"The U.N. treaty system definitively establishes the legitimacy of international interest in the protection of human rights."*

International Human Rights Treaties Are Necessary to Help Prevent Human Rights Abuses

Anne Bayefsky

In the following viewpoint, Anne Bayefsky asserts that the United Nations (UN) treaty system provides a means for individual nations to positively impact the human rights of people the world over. Bayefsky says the UN treaty system provides human rights standards and obligations that nations voluntarily accept. In so doing, nations acquire a legal duty to protect against, prevent, and remedy human rights violations. Anne Bayefsky is an author and professor at York University in Toronto, Canada.

As you read, consider the following questions:

1. Treaty standards are a benchmark for what?
2. How many major treaties are contained in the U.N. Human Rights Treaty System? Name one.

Anne Bayefsky, "Introduction to the UN Human Rights Treaty System," *www.bayefsky.com*. Reproduced by permission.-

3. Describe one of the three different methods mentioned in the viewpoint in which treaty bodies fulfill their monitoring function.

The U.N. [United Nations] treaty system definitively establishes the legitimacy of international interest in the protection of human rights. It is undisputed that sovereignty is limited with respect to human rights. International supervision is valid and states are accountable to international authorities for domestic acts affecting human rights. The treaty standards are the benchmark for assessment and concern.

Over the last decade ratifications in the treaty system and acceptance of communication procedures have risen exponentially. What began as an assertion of a few, is now a global proclamation of entitlements of the victims of human rights abuse. Furthermore, this participation by states has been voluntary. The obligations of the human rights treaties have been freely assumed. It is the legal character of these rights which places them at the core of the international system of human rights protection. For these rights generate corresponding legal duties upon state actors, to protect against, prevent, and remedy human rights violations.

The Goals

The primary aims of the treaty system are to:

- encourage a culture of human rights

- focus the human rights system on standards and obligations

- engage all states in the treaty system

- interpret the treaties through reporting and communications

- identify benchmarks through general comments and recommendations

- provide an accurate, pragmatic, quality end product in the form of concluding observations for each state

- provide a remedial forum for individual complaints

- encourage a serious national process of review and reform through partnerships at the national level

- operationalize standards

- mainstream human rights in the UN system and mobilize the UN community to assist with implementation and the dissemination of the message of rights and obligations

The Standards

The human rights treaty system encompasses seven major treaties:

- the Convention on the Elimination of all forms of Racial Discrimination (in force 4 January 1969)

- the International Covenant on Civil and Political Rights (CCPR) (in force 23 March 1976)

- the International Covenant on Economic, Social and Cultural Rights (in force 23 March 1976)

- the Convention on the Elimination of All Forms of Discrimination Against Women (in force 3 September 1981)

- the Convention Against Torture, and Other Cruel, Inhuman or Degrading Treatment or Punishment (in force 26 June 1987)

- the Convention on the Rights of the Child (in force 2 September 1990)

- the International Convention on the Protection of the Rights of All Migrant Workers and Members of Their Families (in force 1 July 2003).

The Treaty Bodies

The seven treaties are associated with seven treaty bodies which have the task of monitoring the implementation of treaty obligations. Six of the seven treaty bodies meet primarily in Geneva, and are serviced by the Office of the UN High Commissioner for Human Rights (OHCHR). These are:

- the Committee on the Elimination of Racial Discrimination (CERD)

- the Human Rights Committee (HRC)

- the Committee on Economic, Social and Cultural Rights (CESCR)

- the Committee Against Torture (CAT)

- the Committee on the Rights of the Child (CRC)

- the Committee on Migrant Workers (CMW).

One treaty body meets in New York and is serviced by the UN Division for the Advancement of Women:

- the Committee on the Elimination of Discrimination Against Women (CEDAW).

The treaty bodies are composed of members who are elected by the states parties to each treaty (or through the UN Economic and Social Council (ECOSOC) in the case of CESCR). In principle, treaty members are elected as experts who are to perform their functions in an independent capacity.

The Functions of the Treaty Bodies

Meeting periodically throughout the year, the treaty bodies fulfill their monitoring function through one or more of three different methods.

Protecting Human Rights Under the Rule of Law

Both security and prosperity depend on respect for human rights and the rule of law. Throughout history human life has been enriched by diversity, and different communities have learned from each other. But if our communities are to live in peace we must stress also what unites us: our common humanity and the need for our human dignity and rights to be protected by law.

That is vital for development, too. Both foreigners and a country's own citizens are more likely to invest when their basic rights are protected and they know they will be fairly treated under the law. Policies that genuinely favor development are more likely to be adopted if the people most in need of development can make their voice heard. States need to play by the rules toward each other, as well. No community suffers from too much rule of law; many suffer from too little—and the international community is among them.

Kofi Annan, "What I've Learned,"
Washington Post, *December 11, 2006.*

First, all states parties are required by the treaties to produce state reports on the compliance of domestic standards and practices with treaty rights. These reports are reviewed at various intervals by the treaty bodies, normally in the presence of state representatives. Concluding observations, commenting on the adequacy of state compliance with treaty obligations, are issued by the treaty bodies following the review.

Second, in the case of four treaties individuals may complain of violations of their rights under the treaty (the Civil and Political Covenant, the Racial Discrimination Convention, the Convention Against Torture, and the Women's Discrimination Convention). These complaints are considered by the treaty body which expresses a view as to the presence or absence of a violation.

Third, in the case of CAT and CEDAW, their work includes another procedure. This is an inquiry procedure which provides for missions to states parties in the context of concerns about systematic or grave violations of treaty rights.

In addition, the treaty bodies contribute to the development and understanding of international human rights standards through the process of writing General Comments or Recommendations. These are commentaries on the nature of obligations associated with particular treaty rights and freedoms.

The National Level

Significantly, the international system has had implications at the national level. A multitude of domestic legal systems have been affected by the treaties. The treaties form the basis of a significant number of the world's bills of rights. There are also numerous instances of legal reform prompted by the treaties. Non-governmental organizations and national human rights institutions have invoked the treaty standards in relation to proposed government legislation and policies. Legislative committees have used treaty standards as reference points. The treaties have sometimes been incorporated into national law, had direct application through constitutional provisions to national law, and been used to interpret domestic law through judicial intervention.

"There is no evidence that ratification of human rights treaties affects human rights practices."

International Human Rights Laws and Treaties Have Little Impact on Ending Human Rights Abuses

Jack L. Goldsmith and Eric Posner

In this viewpoint, Jack Goldsmith and Eric Posner contend that the United Nations' treaty system is ineffective in preventing or ending human rights abuses largely because the treaties carry no enforcement mechanisms so nations do not suffer any inconveniences when they violate them. Goldsmith and Posner say any improvements in human rights since World War II are due to other factors. The evidence shows that the United Nations' treaties do not change the behaviors of human rights violating states. Jack Goldsmith and Eric Posner are authors and professors at the University of Chicago Law School.

As you read, consider the following questions:

1. Why don't modern human rights treaties reflect asymmetric human rights law?

2. How have television and the Internet affected human rights?

3. According to Goldsmith and Posner, why did human rights violations decline in Uruguay, Paraguay, Honduras, and Argentina?

The modern human rights treaties do not reflect asymmetric human rights law akin to the [1807] British slave treaties, for they do not involve human rights—abiding states offering anything of substance in return for better human rights practices in other states. Rather, the treaties require all states, regardless of their domestic orientation, to do the same thing: treat people under their control well. The treaties also do not reflect symmetric human rights cooperation. Unlike in the [1648] Treaties of Westphalia, the parties' symmetrical actions do not involve meaningful reciprocity. For these reasons, we are skeptical about whether modern human rights treaties reflect robust cooperation. . . .

No Enforcement

The modern human rights treaties [do not] have an effective or reliable coercive enforcement mechanism. The treaties' reporting obligations are their least onerous provisions, and yet states do not appear to take seriously their obligation to submit reports. More than 70 percent of parties have overdue reports; at least 110 states have five or more overdue reports; about 25 percent have initial overdue reports; the mean length of time for an overdue report is five years; and most of these reports are pro forma descriptions of domestic law, and thus not genuine examples of compliance (which would involve the description of human rights violations). The treaties do set up committees that can entertain and respond to petitions by in-

Little Hope That Human Suffering Will End Anytime Soon

We still want our lattes from Starbucks and our nice houses with Direct TV and plasma screens while others are starving and living impoverished lives, not only in other countries but right in our own communities. And we learn to live with the guilt and to reduce, but never eliminate, the cognitive dissonance of this by pointing out that we have the right to the fruits of our hard labor and thus our property. And if that does not work, we are quick to blame the victims, noting that there are practical problems to solving these issues: aid will only be wasted, used for war, or end up in the Swiss bank accounts of corrupt officials.

With the developed countries controlling the Security Council and determining to a large extent not only the content of international law but also how it is implemented, there is little hope that the fundamental economic inequalities that result in so much human suffering around the globe will be addressed anytime soon. Until such inequalities are addressed, however, the idealistic vision of the human-rights movement will remain but one more in a long series of utopian dreams, capable of improving enough people's lives to comfort us that we are making moral progress, while at the same time undermining or inhibiting the development of new vocabularies and, at least in some cases, giving rise to its own form of repression and intolerance.

Randall Peerenboom,
"Human Rights, China, and Cross-Cultural Inquiry:
Philosophy, History, and Power Politics,"
Philosophy East and West, *April 2005, pp. 283–320.*

dividuals. But the recommendations of these committees have no legal force. Perhaps the best indication of the failure of this system is that although 1.4 billion people have the formal right under these treaties to file complaints against their governments, there are only about sixty complaints per year. Beyond these enforcement mechanisms internal to the treaty, states do not coerce other states into complying with the modern multilateral human rights treaties. States do occasionally coerce other states to improve their human rights practices, but this enforcement is episodic and correlates with the coercing state's strategic interest. Violation of a human rights treaty is neither a necessary nor a sufficient condition for being the target of sanctions motivated by concern about human rights violations.

Two conclusions follow. First, a state incurs little if any cost from violating the treaties. Human rights—abusing states can ratify the treaties with little fear of adverse consequences. Second, for other states the human rights treaties do not require changes in behavior: states comply with the treaties for reasons having to do with domestic law and culture independent of the terms of the treaty.

Evidence Says Treaties Do Not Change Behavior

The scant available empirical evidence is consistent with these conclusions. In addition to the treaty-reporting statistics described above, human rights reports issued by the U.S. State Department, Amnesty International, and Human Rights Watch make clear that human rights abuses in violation of the IC-CPR [International Covenant on Civil and Political Rights] are widespread. These reports suggest that the human rights treaties have not had a large impact, but they say nothing about human rights treaties' possible marginal influence on human rights practices. Two quantitative studies address this latter issue. Linda Camp Keith [political science professor] examined the relationship between accession to the ICCPR and the degree of respect for human rights. Oona Hathaway [professor of law] examined the relationship between accession to the entire array of modern human rights treaties and the degree of respect for human rights covered by these treaties. Both studies find no statistically significant relationship, and Hathaway argues that the relationship in some cases is actually negative. To be sure, one reason for these results might be the difficulty of measuring human rights violations, which are hard to detect and to code. Another reason is that liberal states that object to human rights abuses and are willing to devote resources to ending them do not distinguish between human rights abusers that have ratified human rights treaties and those that have not, a point that we develop below. The bottom line remains, however, that there is no evidence that ratification of human rights treaties affects human rights practices. By contrast, empirical studies do fund statistical relationships between democracy, peace, and economic development, on the one hand, and protection of human rights, on the other.

Improvements Due to Other Factors

The conclusion that the modern human rights treaties have had no significant impact on human rights protection is entirely consistent with human rights being more salient today than sixty years ago, with states respecting human rights in ways they might not have earlier, and with a general improvement of human rights since World War II. Increases in international trade and democratization clearly have had an impact on human rights protection during this period. The end of the cold war was probably the event that had the greatest impact on human rights in the past quarter century. The collapse of the Soviet Union enabled long-oppressed domestic polities throughout Eastern Europe and elsewhere to acquire individual freedoms. In addition, changes in technology have affected human rights enforcement. States have always been willing to pay, but not willing to pay much, to relieve visible suffering in other countries, regardless of what human rights law required. Developments since World War II have increased the benefits and lowered the costs of such enforcement. The rise of television and the Internet has made suffering in other countries more visible; ordinary altruists thus gain more by relieving such suffering than in the past, when relief as well as suffering could (at best) be described only in print. Advances in military technology have reduced the cost of intervening when human rights abuses occur in poor states. So, too, have international institutions that were created to facilitate coordination of security issues, which are also available to coordinate responses to human rights abuse. For example, NATO, a security organization constituted by treaty, lowered the coordination and response costs of intervening to stop human rights abuses in the former Yugoslavia in the summer of 1999.

Case Studies Also Show Treaties Have No Effect

Additional support for these arguments comes from case studies that provide detailed information about the relationship between international human rights law and the human rights practices of specific states. One prominent study by [Ellen] Lutz and [Kathryn] Sikkink in 2000 examines three cases from Latin America from the 1970s through the early 1990s. The first two cases involved torture in Uruguay and Paraguay and disappearances in Honduras and Argentina. For each pair, the first state had signed a relevant human rights treaty (the IC-CPR and the American Convention on Human Rights, respectively) prior to the human rights violations in question, and the second state had not. For each pair, background conditions were relatively similar, and each state was a dictatorship when the human rights violations occurred. One might have expected Lutz and Sikkink to find that the signatory state engaged in fewer human rights violations than the nonsignatory state did. In fact, human rights violations declined in both states in each pair at roughly the same time, for roughly the same reason: increased international attention to the human rights practices of the two states, followed by a new U.S. policy under the Carter administration, supported by Congress, to withdraw aid from governments that violated human rights. Neither the activists and journalists who highlighted the human rights abuses nor the Carter administration distinguished between signatories and nonsignatories. And the Carter administration's pressure against all four countries was sufficient to reduce human rights violations where they occurred. Public concern followed by coercion, not the human rights treaties, is the explanatory factor here.

Periodical Bibliography

The following articles have been selected to supplement the diverse views presented in this chapter.

Kofi Annan
"All States Need to Play by the Rules," *New African*, January 2007.

Jimmy Carter
"Human Rights Commission Must Change," *San Francisco Chronicle*, January 2006.

Larry Cox and Dorothy Thomas
"Is the U.S. Ready for Human Rights? Yes. We're Ready." *YesMagazine.org*, Spring 2007.

The Economist
"Great Expectations; Human Rights and the UN," March 24, 2007.

Richard Holbrooke
"Defying Orders, Saving Lives: Heroic Diplomats of the Holocaust," *Foreign Affairs*, May–June 2007.

Alex Kingsury
"Trying One, Blaming Many," *U.S. News & World Report* December 1, 2006.

New York Times
"Armies of Children: The International Criminal Court is Now Drawing Attention to a Widespread, Yet Widely Ignored Horror: The Recruitment of Child Soldiers," October 12, 2006.

Terry O'Neill
"Siding with the Bully: The UN's Human Rights Mandarin Defends the Offence and Offends the Defence." *Western Standard*, January 15, 2007.

Michael Posner
"The Rule of Law," *Boston Globe*, July 18, 2006.

Marlise Simons
"The Struggle for Iraq; Hussein's Case Won't Bolster International Human Rights Law, Experts Fear," *New York Times*, December 31, 2006.

CHAPTER 4

What Human Rights Policies Should the U.S. Government Follow?

Chapter Preface

In the immediate aftermath of September 11, 2001, President [George W.] Bush called on the U.S. Congress to grant him and his administration new powers he said were needed to address terrorism. On October 26, 2001, the president and the Congress enacted the Uniting and Strengthening America by Providing Appropriate Tools Required for the Intervention and Obstruction of Terrorism Act (USA PATRIOT Act), which dramatically expanded the authority of U.S. law enforcement agencies for the purpose of fighting terrorism in the United States and abroad. President Bush and the U.S. Congress believe that the USA PATRIOT Act is necessary to protect Americans against terrorism. However, many human rights groups believe that the USA Patriot Act undermines the rights of Americans and noncitizens and weakens the framework for promoting human rights internationally.

After the September 11, 2001, attacks the U.S. government was eager to show Americans and the world that the United States was going to do all it could to prevent another attack from occurring on U.S. soil. Knowing that the perpetrators of the 9/11 attacks had planned the attacks—and trained for them by taking flying lessons—while living and working in the United States infuriated many Americans. Among its many provisions, the USA Patriot Act increases the ability of law enforcement agencies to search telephone and e-mail communications and medical, financial, and other records; eases restrictions on foreign intelligence gathering within the United States; expands the secretary of the treasury's authority to regulate financial transactions, particularly those involving foreign individuals and entities; and enhances the discretion of law enforcement and immigration authorities in detaining and deporting immigrants suspected of terrorism. The USA Patriot Act was enacted in response to many of the perceived shortcomings of U.S. government policy that allowed 9/11 attackers to live and work in the United States while plotting to bring terror to U.S. soil.

Many people have criticized the USA Patriot Act because they believe it tramples on Americans' right to privacy and other civil liberties and it denies basic human rights to immigrants and foreign-born nationals. Groups like the American Civil Liberties Union (ACLU) are concerned with the impact of the act's information-gathering provisions on privacy. Says the ACLU, "There are significant flaws in the Patriot Act, flaws that threaten your fundamental freedoms by giving the government the power to access your medical records, tax records, and information about the books you buy or borrow without probable cause, and the power to break into your home and conduct secret searches without telling you for weeks, months, or indefinitely." Others are concerned about the act's immigration provisions, which allow the government broad discretion to detain foreign nationals. Says Georgetown University law professor David Cole, "the rights we're denying are human rights, not privileges of citizenship. They're not limited to citizens. They extend to all. It's counterproductive because it contributes to the rising tide of anti-Americanism around the world, which I see as the greatest threat to national security that we face." The ACLU, Professor Cole, and others believe that the USA Patriot Act erodes civil and human rights without keeping the United States any safer.

But others believe that the Patriot Act is necessary to keep America safe from terrorists. President Bush, speaking in 2005, said, "Over the past three-and-a-half years, America's law enforcement and intelligence personnel have proved that the Patriot Act works. . . . Federal, state, and local law enforcement have used the Patriot Act to break up terror cells in New York and Oregon and Virginia and in Florida. . . . The Patriot Act has accomplished exactly what it was designed to do—it has protected American liberty, and saved American lives." Supporters of the Patriot Act say it has built-in provisions to protect individual rights, and it only gives investigators the ability to fight terror, using many of the same court-approved tools that have been used successfully for many years in drug fraud and organized crime cases. Many Patriot Act supporters also contend that when it comes to keeping America safe, some trade offs are necessary. Says conservative columnist Michelle Malkin, "Civil liberties extremists pretend there are no tradeoffs, no costs, to putting legal absolutism over national security. That is simply not the case." Bush, Malkin, and others believe that sacrificing some rights and freedoms may be necessary in order to keep America safe.

The USA Patriot Act was set to expire on December 31, 2005, but was reauthorized on March 2, 2006. Fourteen of the USA Patriot Act's sixteen provisions are now permanent and the other two will expire, unless reauthorized again, in 2010. The debate about the USA Patriot Act is one of many debates concerning U.S. government policy and human rights issues. The authors in the following chapter discuss the human rights policies they believe the U.S. government should follow.

> "The Court's aims and objectives dem-
> onstrate that the ICC shares similar
> values and moral history that America
> was founded upon, and that common
> ground exists both for the Court and
> U.S. acceptance of it."

The United States Should Be a Part of the International Criminal Court

Briony MacPhee

In the following viewpoint, Briony MacPhee contends that the goals and objectives of the International Criminal Court (ICC) are consistent with conservative American values and the United States should participate in the court. The United States played a key role in drafting some of the documents establishing the ICC, but citing concerns that American service members could be subject to investigation or prosecution, the United States has not joined it. This is the wrong conclusion, says MacPhee, and she addresses this and other concerns of U.S. conservatives. Bri-

Briony MacPhee, "The International Criminal Court: A Case for Conservatives," *The American Non-Governmental Organizations Coalition for the International Criminal Court (AMICC)*, August 30, 2005, www.amicc.org/docs/Case%20for%20Conservatives .pdf. Reproduced by permission of the publisher and the author.

ony MacPhee, is a professional volunteer associate with the American Non-Governmental Organizations Coalition for the International Criminal Court.

As you read, consider the following questions:

1. Which countries were among the first to refer situations to the ICC?

2. List the concerns that conservatives have with U.S. participation in the ICC, as stated in the viewpoint.

3. In regard to the worldwide deployment of American servicemen and -women, what does Article 98 of the Rome Statute require?

Since negotiations began on the first permanent International Criminal Court (ICC or Court) in 1995, conservatives in the United States have been concerned about its creation and its implications for American sovereignty and international actions. This range of concerns has led many conservatives to conclude that the Court does not merit U.S. support and involvement.

This [viewpoint] examines the important concerns that conservative Americans have expressed regarding the ICC, and responds to them. Close examination of the Court indicates that the values that are important to conservatives are implemented and carried out by the ICC.

The ICC in Operation

On July 1, 2002, the ICC came into existence following the necessary 60th ratification of its Rome Statute, with jurisdiction over crimes committed after this date. The ICC advances global peace through internationally administered justice. It is unprecedented as a permanent tribunal to try individuals, regardless of nationality, for the most serious crimes, including genocide, crimes against humanity, war crimes, and when defined, the crime of aggression. The states which support the

ICC are democratic and free, thus the judges elected will be from democratic countries, as evidenced in those that have been elected so far. Moreover, the staff of the ICC is drawn from countries all over the world, both members and non-members of the Court. For example, an American is a senior prosecutor, responsible for managing the Uganda case.

The ICC is up and running, with the support of nearly 100 countries that have ratified the Rome Statute. The governments of the Democratic Republic of the Congo (DRC), Uganda and the Central African Republic (CAR) are among the first to refer situations to the ICC. In addition, the United Nations Security Council has referred the situation in Darfur (Sudan) to the ICC, and the Ivory Coast has consented to the Court's jurisdiction. Investigations have already begun in the DRC, Uganda and Darfur, and arrest warrants are expected soon. . . .

History and Creation of the ICC

The sheer scale of horror committed during the Holocaust made the international community brutally aware of the power of ethnic hate, and the evil of leaders who are not called to account for planning and creating atrocities. American troops led the effort to liberate Nazi concentration camps, playing a noble role to end the atrocities. The United States also led the effort to establish the subsequent Nuremberg and Tokyo tribunals, holding the perpetrators to account, and helping to establish the principle of individual accountability for war crimes.

Although "never again" was the battle cry after World War II, the success of the Nuremberg and Tokyo tribunals did not lead to the establishment of a permanent court to try such crimes. The Cold War made it impossible politically to create a court. The consequences of this failure are apparent in the recent atrocities committed in Sierra Leone, Rwanda, East Timor, and the former Yugoslavia, along with other cases. The ad hoc tribunals were the pilot project, but their experiences made it evident that a permanent court was needed and that the UN Security Council could not create it.

The motives of other countries and their historical experiences were among the factors that led to the creation of the ICC. Many countries who drafted the Rome Statute recently emerged from dictatorships to democracy. It was their unstable and violent past, coupled with the desire to have a permanent court to deal with atrocities that continue to happen around the world, which led them to create the Court.

The experience of the ad hoc tribunals also motivated the creation of the ICC. Although there have been difficulties with their operation, the tribunals have worked. Currently more than 50 individuals have been prosecuted and are serving sentences for the crimes they committed in the former Yugoslavia and Rwanda. This demonstrates that tribunals such as these can be successful, but their cost, their temporariness, and their inability to deter continuing crimes because they act only after the atrocities are over, makes the need for a permanent court obvious.

Concerns About U.S. Participation

The ICC implements most American values about trials and justice, and has thus far demonstrated its impartiality, independence and international acceptance. However, in the United States there is still fear and deep doubt about the reach, mandate and operation of the Court. The concerns of conservatives include: that the Court will be able to try and prosecute Americans, that U.S. participation may be unconstitutional, that there will be a loss of American sovereignty, that there is an absence of safeguards, especially when the U.S. is not a party to the Court, that the Court will have the defects of the ad hoc tribunals and finally, that the Court will limit America's ability to act in its national interest.

ICC Prosecution of Americans Unlikely

It is highly unlikely that the Court will ever prosecute Americans. This is partly, but not only, because of the calculated and widespread manner in which the crimes must be committed, and the limited kinds of crimes that the ICC can prosecute. Countries such as America reject and abhor the kind of atrocities that the Court has been created to adjudicate. It is only the tyrannical leaders of countries that repeatedly violate the most fundamental and basic human rights that will be brought before the Court and held to account. The Rome Statute also limits the Court's jurisdiction to individuals who are citizens of a country party to the ICC or who have committed crimes in the territory of such a country. Only if the Security Council refers a case, or a country accepts the Court's jurisdiction, can the ICC act when the states involved are not party to the Court.

In order for an American servicemember to be tried before the ICC, an American would have to commit crimes of the horrible nature described in the Statute, the U.S. would not investigate the crime or a trial by one of the most respected legal systems in the world would be deemed biased by the ICC, neither the U.S. nor its allies could convince the ICC prosecutor not to investigate, and/or the Pre-Trial Chamber of the Court, composed of elected judges, would approve the Prosecutor's decision to investigate. Finally, despite U.S. influence, the Security Council would also have to refuse to defer the investigation, which is under its mandate.

Even if such an unlikely scenario should occur, the accused American would come before a court whose due process requirements are virtually identical to those provided in U.S. courts. These provisions of the Rome Statute are identical to those in the U.S. Bill of Rights. The Statute includes rights such as the right to a speedy trial, the right to remain silent and the right to be questioned with counsel present. The only difference between the rights provided for Americans in U.S.

courts and the ICC is that there is no trial by jury. However, a jury trial for Pol Pot, Idi Amin, Saddam Hussein or Adolf Hitler would be an impractical mockery of the whole meaning and purpose of juries. Who exactly would be the peers of such men? The ICC provides instead for trial by judges schooled in the highest legal principles of the Court, thus ensuring that their rulings will be rooted in them. It is clear that the ICC is not a biased [court], but is rather a court that is founded on the basic rights and privileges awarded to all Americans, ensuring that Americans would receive a proper and fair trial before the ICC.

Participation Does Not Violate Constitution

Some Americans declare that U.S. participation in the ICC will be unconstitutional. They argue that the Court circumvents the powers of Congress to establish the federal judicial system and that an American who has committed a crime in the U.S. cannot be tried in a court located outside of the country, one which Congress neither created nor drafted its rules.

This would not be the first time that the United States would subject its nationals to be tried in a judicial system other than an American one. The U.S. has entered into previous treaties that allow its nationals to be brought before foreign courts. Examples of such extraterritorial judicial reach are the extradition treaties that the U.S. has established and continuously honors with many countries. For example, if an American commits a crime in another country, and the United States has an extradition treaty with that country, the U.S. is obliged to send that person to that country. A state has absolute and exclusive jurisdiction over those who commit crimes within its territory. This has been an accepted concept that has been a part of American law as far back as 1812. Furthermore, Supreme Court cases have made apparent that it is not unconstitutional to try Americans in foreign courts. It is abundantly clear from these cases that Americans can be extradited, and have been extradited, to countries whose judicial systems are very dissimilar to American courts—for example, courts that do not have trial by jury.

The ICC is not the kind of American court in which the Congress is authorized to establish under Article III of the U.S. Constitution. Instead, it is a court outside the U.S. and in that respect is similar to the courts of foreign countries. Therefore, the U.S. is not escaping the Court's jurisdiction if it does not sign onto the ICC. As long as America is not party to the Statute and does not wish to make its nationals available to the Court, the ICC will only be able to prosecute Americans who are physically in foreign nations, which would have primary jurisdiction over them even without the ICC. In fact, given this reach of foreign courts even without American endorsement of the ICC, U.S. membership in the Court may actually serve to increase its influence and clout in such cases.

American Sovereignty Intact

The creation of this Court is not an attempt to check American power, nor a step toward world government. Moral considerations prompted the ICC's formation. The Court was a reaction to a brutal history and a refusal to accept perpetual atrocities. The fact that the ICC was created by a group of nations indicates that it is not an outside institution which simply materialized by its own accord to impose its will on the United States. Rather than violate the principle of sovereignty, the ICC is its expression. It is an act of sovereignty for countries to join treaties and organizations. The countries that drafted the Rome Statute, and subsequently signed and ratified it, are exercising their right to create an international organization. These countries still have the right to legislate and enforce the law within their own borders, and they are encouraged to do so. The Court's restricted jurisdiction is deliberate. . . .

Amnesty International: U.S. Should Join ICC

The United States of America is the only state that is actively opposed to the new International Criminal Court. U.S. opposition to the Court can be traced back to the adoption of the Rome Statute of the International Criminal Court (Rome Statute) in 1998, where the USA was one of only 7 states to vote against adoption of the Statute. Reportedly a major reason for not supporting adoption of the Statute stems from the refusal of the international community to grant the United Nations Security Council (of which the USA is a veto holding permanent member) control over which cases the Court considered, instead favouring an independent Prosecutor who—subject to safeguards and fair trial guarantees—would make such decisions.

On 31 December 2000, however, President [Bill] Clinton signed the Rome Statute, which was a positive step in favour of the Court. However, the U.S. position has changed dramatically since the new administration under President [George W.] Bush took office in 2001. On 6 May 2002, the U.S. government took the unprecedented step of repudiating its signature of the Rome Statute and began a worldwide campaign to weaken the Court and to obtain impunity for all U.S. nationals from the jurisdiction of the Court.

Amnesty International believes that the U.S. concerns that the ICC will be used to bring politically motivated prosecutions against U.S. nationals are wholly unfounded. The substantial safeguards and fair trial guarantees in the Rome Statute will ensure that such a situation would never arise.

Amnesty International,
"U.S. Threats to the International Criminal Court,"
web.amnesty.org.

Safeguards Are Present

Conservatives are worried that the Court does not have the necessary safeguards to prevent politically motivated investigations and prosecutions, especially against Americans. However, the Court only has jurisdiction over "the most serious crimes of concern to the international community as a whole," which necessitates that criminal acts must have occurred on a large scale and be the result of deliberate plans or policies by a nation or organization.

If U.S. enemies do seek to use the ICC to achieve anti-American political objectives, there are numerous safeguards against this. The negotiators of the Rome Statute anticipated attempts to politically pervert the Court and quite wisely took careful precautions to prevent the abuse of the Court for political gain. If used in conjunction, such protections may provide nearly total exemption for any country with a well-functioning legal system.

Perhaps the most significant limitation and check on the Court is that it is a court of last resort. As discussed above, the Court is obliged to defer to national proceedings unless it can be shown that the state with jurisdiction over a case is unable or unwilling to act. Such a state must be notified if the Court is beginning an investigation and therefore has the ability to invoke complementarity to demonstrate that it can try the resulting cases. . . .

ICC Not Like Tribunals

Although previous ad hoc tribunals have helped a great deal in bringing to justice those responsible for the atrocities committed in the former Yugoslavia and Rwanda, they have failed to deter atrocities because they are established only after the crimes they address have been committed. The early corruption of the International Criminal Tribunal for Rwanda, the chaotic start of the International Criminal Tribunal for the former Yugoslavia, and the occasional failure of the tribunals to follow the rules and safeguards in their statutes, are all pointed to as failures of the process. The setbacks of the tribunals came from their improvised nature, lack of a permanent mandate, and inadequate oversight by the Security Council. As each was established, it had to start from scratch in operations, investigations, prosecutions, personnel recruitment and financing.

The permanence of the Court greatly reduces these problems. For example, the Court has its own set of rules and standards for procedure and evidence, personnel recruitment and the election of judges, all of which are carefully discussed and reviewed before approval by the ASP [Assembly of State Parties]. The ability of the ICC to organize itself permanently before its first indictments gives the institution a huge advantage over the ad hoc tribunals. In fact, many of the tribunals' staff were closely involved in ICC negotiations, and some have even been elected to serve as judges or members of the Registry. These individuals can take their past experiences and transform them into positive reinforcement for the Court.

Only Most Serious Crimes Under ICC Jurisdiction

A final concern is that the ICC will inhibit policymakers to act or make choices in the interest of the country. One fear, especially felt by many military officials, is that military operations may constitute crimes against humanity, or, once defined, the crime of aggression. Such concerns are unnecessary because the ICC was not designed to prosecute citizens of democratic countries which normally do not plan and commit atrocities. In fact, it is unthinkable that Americans would ever commit such crimes since they are calculated and strategic, not the collateral damage of warfare.

The crimes under the Court's jurisdiction must be extremely serious and executed as a matter of official policy, within a repeated pattern of abuse. This ensures that only a very particular type of criminal will come before the ICC. The war crimes the Statute describes can be found in the military manuals of the U.S. army and the definitions of their elements were shaped, supported and finally approved by the U.S. and Department of Defense in negotiations on the ICC. The crime of genocide requires the intent to destroy a national, ethnic, racial or religious group. Crimes against humanity and war crimes have to be committed as part of a broad and consistent policy, not an inadvertent act. Therefore the U.S. need not fear prosecution from an error or combat miscalculation. It is unthinkable that a U.S. official would ever commit such crimes. Since the end of World War II, it is arguable that no actions taken by Americans would qualify for the ICC's jurisdiction.

In addition, conservatives should not fear that the worldwide deployment of Americans to serve our country will expose them to the political abuses of the ICC. Article 98 of the Statute provides for protection of U.S. citizens serving in the military or as officials abroad. It requires the ICC to defer to Status of Forces Agreements (SOFAs), which protect U.S. soldiers, sailors, air force personnel and marines abroad, and to Status of Mission Agreements (SOMAs) for U.S. officials. Therefore, it may even be argued that the Court will aid in the protection of Americans, especially servicepersons, because of its many protective provisions.

Concern over possible prosecution for the crime of aggression is understandable. However, there will be jurisdiction over the crime of aggression only when a provision is adopted defining the crime and the conditions for such jurisdiction. If the U.S. ratifies the Statute before such a definition is adopted, it will be able to participate in negotiations surrounding its adoption. As a State Party, the U.S. will also have the right to reject the definition and thus not be bound by the ICC's jurisdiction for this crime. Thus, for the U.S., the jurisdiction of the court can easily remain only war crimes, genocide, and crimes against humanity.

Participation in the ICC Consistent with American Values

Freedom, democracy and equality—these are all profoundly American values upon which the United States was founded. The U.S. should use its strength and influence in the world to support those values on an international scale and thus put its power to good use. Personal accountability and respect for the rule of law is a fundamental value on which America was built, protection of which is also fundamental at the international level.

Many conservatives often support humanitarian efforts to help those in need. They frequently mount substantial efforts to aid individuals victimized by violent conflict, genocide, and political upheaval. Conservatives respect and make sacrifices for the principle that ignoring a mutilated man, a raped woman or a starving child, no matter how far overseas, is a moral outrage. Although the American people overwhelmingly support humanitarian efforts, their resolve is often tested by the substantial costs in American lives and tax dollars. In addition, humanitarian relief efforts rarely lead to a permanent solution. If the ICC does indeed have a deterrent effect, much of the humanitarian work sponsored by the U.S. abroad may no longer be necessary, allowing Americans to continue to advance their humanitarian ideals while potentially avoiding the deaths of American soldiers and rerouting the millions spent on humanitarian aid.

While such efforts are crucial and greatly aid victims, the goal should be to prevent these atrocities when they occur, and to punish the perpetrators. This is the mandate of the ICC. It holds to account individuals that commit horrible acts. Americans fight to end horrible crimes such as human trafficking, slavery, religious persecution and mutilation. Such crimes are included in the jurisdiction of the Court. The Court's aims and objectives demonstrate that the ICC shares similar values and moral history that America was founded upon, and that common ground exists both for the Court and U.S. acceptance of it.

> *"Unless the ICC's flaws are addressed, the United States should not join the court and should oppose initiatives that could give credence to the court's claims of jurisdiction over American nationals and military."*

The United States Should Not Be a Part of the International Criminal Court

Brett D. Schaefer

In the following viewpoint, Brett D. Schaefer says the U.S. policy is correct: We should not join the International Criminal Court (ICC). Schaefer says the ICC lacks safeguards against political manipulation, is not accountable to the United Nations (UN) Security Council, and violates national sovereignty. Schaefer believes the United States should protect Americans using Article 98 agreements and oppose UN resolutions seeking to legitimize the ICC. Brett Schaefer is a fellow at the Center for International Trade and Economics at The Heritage Foundation.

Brett D. Schaefer, "The Bush Administration's Policy on the International Criminal Court Is Correct," *Backgrounder*, March 8, 2005. Copyright © 2005 The Heritage Foundation. Reproduced by permission.

As you read, consider the following questions:

1. Criticism of U.S. policy toward the ICC has specifically targeted the ASPA and the Nethercutt amendment. What do these laws do?

2. What are Article 98 agreements?

3. How many countries has America concluded Article 98 agreements with? Is this more or less than the number that have ratified or acceded to the Rome Statute?

The United States and many advocates for the International Criminal Court (ICC) have long been at odds over the court's statute, accountability, and jurisdiction. Although these differences have not been resolved, two recent actions have refocused international and domestic attention on America's policy toward the ICC. The first was enactment of the Nethercutt amendment, which extended prohibitions on assistance to ICC parties beyond those already in place under the American Servicemembers' Protection Act (ASPA). The second is the debate over whether or not the U.N. [United Nations] Security Council should refer the genocide in Sudan to the ICC for investigation.

As with earlier disagreements over U.S. policy toward the ICC, advocates of the court seek to portray the U.S. position as shortsighted and at odds with human rights. Nothing could be further from the truth.

Both the [Bill] Clinton Administration and the [George W.] Bush Administration concluded that the ICC is a seriously flawed institution that the U.S. should not join. Regrettably, the Rome Statute establishing the ICC broke with long-standing international legal precedent by asserting ICC jurisdiction over nationals and military personnel from states that are not party to the treaty. This forced the U.S. to take unusual steps to protect its people from the ICC.

Unless the ICC's flaws are addressed, the U.S. should not join the court and should oppose initiatives that could give credence to the court's claims of jurisdiction over American nationals and military. . . .

History of American Policy Toward ICC

America has long been a champion of human rights. It was a key supporter of the ad hoc war crimes tribunals in Rwanda and the former Yugoslavia, which were approved by the Security Council. It was an eager participant in the effort to create the International Criminal Court. Once negotiations began on the final version of the Rome Statute, however, America's concerns were ignored and the final document was approved despite U.S. opposition.

Since the approval of the Rome Statute, U.S. policy toward the ICC has been clear and consistent: The U.S. opposes the ICC because it is an international legal body that lacks prudent safeguards against political manipulation, possesses sweeping authority without accountability to the Security Council, and violates national sovereignty by claiming jurisdiction over the nationals and military personnel of non-party states.

The U.S. policy toward the ICC was initiated by the Clinton Administration—a fact that is conveniently ignored by ICC advocates. According to former Ambassador-at-Large for War Crimes Issues David J. Scheffer, the 1998 negotiations on the Rome Statute "produced a seriously flawed take-it-or-leave-it text, one that provides a recipe for politicization of the court and risks deterring responsible international action to promote peace and security." Although acknowledging the treaty's "significant flaws" and recommending to his successor against submitting the treaty to the Senate for advice and consent, President Bill Clinton signed the ICC treaty in December 2000 to give the U.S. an opportunity to address American concerns.

After several ineffective attempts to change the objectionable parts of the ICC treaty, the Bush Administration ended the farce of the U.S. being a signatory to a treaty that it would never ratify by sending a letter to the U.N. Secretary-General declaring that "the United States has no legal obligations arising from its signature" of the Rome Statute—in essence, "unsigning" the Rome Statute.

In normal circumstances, this would have ended the matter; but the ICC, in direct contravention of the norms and precedents of international law, claims jurisdiction to prosecute and imprison persons from countries that are not party to the Rome Statute and, more shockingly, jurisdiction over those who have specifically rejected the court's jurisdiction. This unprecedented break with international legal norms has required the U.S. to take unusual steps to protect its citizens and military personnel by:

- Blocking overzealous advocates of the ICC from using the Security Council to legitimize the ICC's illegitimate claims of jurisdiction and

- Protecting U.S. citizens and military personnel through a network of Article 98 agreements (non-surrender agreements named after the section of the ICC treaty that permits such arrangements) with as many countries as possible. Countries that sign such agreements with the United States promise, in effect, not to surrender U.S. nationals or military personnel to the ICC without the consent of the U.S. government.

Even though the Bush Administration policy is benign, focused solely on shielding the U.S. from the ICC and not designed to undermine the court, it has been met with hostility by supporters of the court.

Article 98 Agreements

Criticism of U.S. policy toward the ICC has specifically targeted the ASPA and the Nethercutt amendment. These laws, respectively, prohibit disbursement of U.S. military assistance and economic support funds to countries that are party to the Rome Statute unless they are specifically exempted in the legislation, have entered into an Article 98 agreement with the U.S., or have received a waiver from the President.

Critics object to the non-surrender agreements and to using U.S. foreign assistance as a means for convincing countries to sign the agreements. These criticisms mischaracterize U.S. policy:

Article 98: Limited in Scope, Consistent with International Law

Article 98 agreements are limited in scope. Critics see Article 98 agreements as a direct threat to the ICC or as "bilateral immunity agreements." This is a great exaggeration. The agreements are nothing more than an obligation by the country not to turn U.S. persons over to the ICC without permission from the U.S. government. They do not absolve the U.S. of its obligation to investigate and prosecute alleged crimes or constrain the other nation's ability to investigate and prosecute crimes committed by an American person within its jurisdiction. Finally, the agreements do not constrain the ability of an international tribunal established by the Security Council to investigate or prosecute crimes committed by American persons. The Article 98 agreements simply prevent U.S. persons from being turned over to an international legal body that does not have jurisdiction recognized by the U.S.

The limited nature of Article 98 agreements is entirely consistent with international law, which supports the principle that a state cannot be bound by a treaty to which it is not a party. The agreements are also consistent with customary

Unsigning the ICC Treaty

The Bush administration unsigned it [treaty to establish the International Criminal Count], which is an unusual step to take in international law. Basically, what happens is that over the course of many administrations, there are lots of treaties the United States signs but does not submit or plan to submit for advice and consent to ratification—in other words, for Senate approval. And, so long as it's on hold, the treaty has a certain standing in international law under the *Vienna Convention on the Law of Treaties*, and that standing is that if you have signed it but haven't ratified it, you have certain international obligations with respect to the treaty and that goes to the issue of not defeating the object and purpose of the agreement.

If you go so far as to un-sign it, what that means is that not only is it on indefinite hold, the executive has made a decision to actively remove it from the queue. That changes your relationship to the agreement under international law under the Vienna Convention, so you no longer have even that minimal obligation under the treaty and its object and purpose.

Lee Feinstein and Mary Crane,
"Interview with Lee Feinstein on the International Criminal Court
and the United States,"
Council on Foreign Relations, *October 5, 2005,www.cfr.org.*

international law because the issue of ICC jurisdiction is very much in dispute. Moreover, they are consistent with the Rome Statute itself, which permits such agreements in Article 98 of the treaty.

Foreign Aid Has Been Used for Persuasion

Countries are not entitled to U.S. assistance. The U.S. can assign any conditions to its assistance that it deems appropriate and often does so, as demonstrated by the many laws and congressional earmarks governing disbursement of foreign assistance. The U.S. distributes most assistance, particularly military assistance and economic support funds, to support U.S. policy priorities.

Congress and the Administration have determined through the ASPA and the Nethercutt amendment that protecting U.S. persons from the illegitimate claims of ICC jurisdiction is an American priority. Congress has also determined that this concern generally supersedes other foreign aid priorities, but has provided a waiver to the President for any exceptions.

Constraints on foreign assistance have been useful in persuading countries to sign Article 98 agreements. The constraints provide a reason (i.e., maintaining eligibility for U.S. assistance) for countries to sign the Article 98 agreements in the face of aggressive financial and other pressure from the European Union, the United Nations, and ICC advocacy groups.

However, the critics of the U.S. policy are exaggerating the legislation's impact. . . . In truth, the ASPA and Nethercutt restrictions are far less intrusive than other constraints on U.S. foreign assistance. For instance, they do not force a country either to adopt strict labor or environmental standards or to restructure fiscal priorities. They do not even demand that a country not become a party to the ICC. They simply ask the country to respect the sovereign decision of the U.S. not to be a party.

ICC Unlikely to Help in Darfur

Critics are similarly mischaracterizing the U.S. objection to U.N. Security Council resolutions referencing the ICC, such as a recommendation that the ICC investigate accusations of genocide, war crimes, and crimes against humanity in Darfur,

Sudan. The U.S. has been leading the effort to stop atrocities around the world, particularly in Darfur. Specifically:

- While serving as Secretary of State, Colin Powell declared that violations of human rights, war crimes, and genocide were occurring.

- The U.S. led the effort to pass a Security Council resolution condemning the atrocities and has pressed for economic sanctions on Sudan because of the government's support for militia groups committing atrocities in Darfur.

- The U.S. has been a key supporter of the African Union peacekeepers authorized by the Security Council to monitor the situation.

- The U.S. is a major donor of humanitarian aid to people in the region, providing over $567 million in aid since 2003.

- The U.S. has consistently insisted that those responsible for the atrocities in Darfur must be held to account by an ad hoc tribunal.

The U.S. has been frustrated in its effort. The Security Council has not imposed sanctions because China, France, and Russia—afraid that their commercial interests would suffer—have threatened to veto resolutions imposing sanctions. The U.N. Human Rights Commission has minimized criticism of Sudan because that nation sits on the commission.

The U.S. has not drawn the ire of human rights and ICC advocacy groups because it opposes an investigation into the atrocities in Darfur. What angers the ICC advocates is that the U.S. opposes using the ICC to investigate the atrocities in Darfur. The fact is that ICC advocates have focused attention away from the true failure—the inability to pass a Security Council resolution imposing sanctions if Sudan fails to constrain the militia groups—onto U.S. opposition to a Security Council resolution requesting that the ICC investigate atrocities in Darfur.

Worse, the ICC advocates are dismissive of valid reasons for establishing an ad hoc tribunal. From the U.S. perspective, using the ICC would undermine ongoing efforts to build regional capacity among Africans to handle conflicts and hold accountable those who commit atrocities. As noted by international lawyers Lee Casey and David Rivkin:

> [B]oth of the ICC's current investigations involve African countries, the Democratic Republic of Congo and Uganda, respectively. Adding Darfur to this list begins to look a very great deal like European justice for African defendants.

Subsequent announcements that the ICC intends to look at cases in the Central African Republic and the Ivory Coast bolster that argument.

Moreover, the ICC lacks an enforcement mechanism and would face many challenges in arresting and incarcerating perpetrators, since Khartoum [capital of Sudan] would be unlikely to assist the court. A regional solution based on an African Union and U.N. hybrid court approved by the Security Council—perhaps using the existing infrastructure of the International Criminal Tribunal for Rwanda in Arusha, Tanzania—could count on support from the existing African Union forces to support the arrest and incarceration of the perpetrators and serve as the core of a permanent African Union court of justice, which is a goal of that body.

The bottom line is that, while it is opposed to a Security Council resolution supporting an ICC investigation in Darfur, the U.S. has proposed a credible—even superior—alternative. The fact that ICC advocates are angered by the U.S. proposal reveals that they are more interested in affirming the authority of the ICC through the Security Council than they are in seeing justice done.

What the United States Should Do

The U.S. has decided that the flaws in the Rome Statute are serious enough to prohibit U.S. participation in the International Criminal Court. Unless these flaws are addressed, the U.S. should not join the court and should oppose initiatives that could give credence to the court's claims of jurisdiction over American nationals and military personnel. Specifically, the U.S. should:

- *Continue to use the ASPA and the Nethercutt amendment as tools to secure Article 98 agreements.* Despite the best efforts of pro-ICC countries and groups, America has concluded Article 98 agreements with 99 governments—more than the number of countries that have ratified or acceded to the Rome Statute. Significantly, over two-thirds of these agreements are with ICC parties and signatories. The ASPA and the Nethercutt amendment have contributed to this progress, and U.S. negotiators should use them to convince other countries to sign Article 98 agreements with the U.S.

- *Oppose Security Council resolutions endorsing the International Criminal Court or referring cases— including the Darfur atrocities in Sudan—to the ICC.* The United States has been a leader in trying to force the Sudanese government to stop supporting the militia groups that are committing atrocities in Darfur. The Security Council's failure to impose sanctions on the Sudanese government despite the best efforts of the U.S. government is a tragedy that sadly reveals the failures of the U.N. in dealing with human rights abuses. The fact that commercial interests in China, France, and Russia trump efforts to stop genocide is shameful. ICC advocates, however, have ignored these true failures and instead have focused attention on U.S. opposition to the ICC. In truth, the U.S. fully supports establishing a tribunal to address allegations of war crimes, human rights abuses, and genocide. America has proposed a solution that will address the situation without compromising America's policy toward the ICC. The ICC advocates need to decide whether their allegiance to the court is more important than the need to see that justice is done in Darfur.

U.S. Can Do Better than the ICC

The true measure of America's commitment to peace and justice and its opposition to genocide and war crimes lies not in its participation in international bureaucracies like the ICC, but in its actions. The United States has led the fight to free millions in Afghanistan and Iraq. It is a party to many human rights treaties and, unlike many other nations, abides by those treaty commitments.

The U.S. has led the charge to hold violators of human rights to account, including fighting hard for imposing Security Council sanctions on the Sudanese government until it stops supporting the militia groups that are committing genocide in Darfur and helps to restore order to the region. The U.S. polices its military and punishes them when they commit crimes. In every practical way, the U.S. honors the beliefs and purposes underlying the ICC.

But America's strong record on human rights is irrelevant to advocates of the ICC. Supporters of the court appear more interested in whether or not a country is a party to the Rome Statute than in whether or not the country actually lives up to the principles of the ICC treaty.

For instance, over 150 allegations of sexual abuse have been made against the civilian and military personnel deployed on the U.N. peacekeeping mission in the Democratic

Republic of the Congo—including persons from a number of ICC parties—but few prosecutions or investigations are ongoing. ICC supporters' time would be better spent in pressing these countries to hold their nationals and military to account or urging ICC signatories Iran, Sudan, Zimbabwe, and Russia to address human rights concerns in their countries—violations that range from substandard to horrifying.

> *"The risks to American values if we fail to act against genocide are far greater than the risks to American interests if we act against it."*

The United States Should Intervene in Darfur

The New Republic

In this viewpoint, the editors of The New Republic *assert that the United States should use military force to end the genocide in Darfur. There is no other reasonable solution, say the editors, and anyone who thinks the United Nations can end the atrocities is sadly mistaken. The editors of* The New Republic *point a finger at those who wring their hands over the bloodshed in Darfur, but who oppose sending in American troops to stop it.* The New Republic *is an American opinion magazine.*

As you read, consider the following questions:

1. Which countries suffered genocides in the 1990s?
2. How long would it take before a United Nations force could be deployed in Darfur?

3. According to *The New Republic* editors, what are
   the reasons that President Bush has been "tepid"
   about Darfur?

Never again? What nonsense. Again and again is more like it. In Darfur, we are witnessing a genocide again, and again we are witnessing ourselves witnessing it and doing nothing to stop it. Even people who wish to know about the problem do not wish to know about the solution. They prefer the raising of consciousnesses to the raising of troops. Just as Rwanda made a bleak mockery of the lessons of Bosnia, Darfur is making a bleak mockery of the lessons of Rwanda. Some lessons, it seems, are gladly and regularly unlearned. Except, of course, by the perpetrators of this evil, who learn the only really enduring lessons about genocide in our time: that the Western response to it is late in coming, or is not coming at all.

Military Force Should Be First Resort Against Evils of Genocide

Were the 1990s really that long ago? They are remembered now as the halcyon and money-happy interval between the war against Soviet totalitarianism and the war against Islamic totalitarianism, but the truth is that, even in the years immediately following the cold war, history never relented. The '90s were a decade of genocides—unimpeded (Rwanda) and partially impeded (Bosnia) and impeded (Kosovo). The relative success of those genocides was owed generally to the indifference of that chimera known as "the international community," but, more specifically, it was owed to the learning curve of an American president about the moral—and therefore the operational—difference between genocide and other foreign policy crises. The difference is simple. In the response to most foreign policy crises, the use of military force is properly viewed as a last resort. In the response to genocide, the use of military force is properly viewed as a first resort.

The notion of force as a first resort defies the foundations of diplomacy and also of common sense: A willingness to use hard power abroad must not become a willingness to use it wildly. But if you are not willing to use force against genocide immediately, then you do not understand what genocide is. Genocide is not a crisis that escalates into evil. It is evil from its inception. It may change in degree if it is allowed to proceed, but it does not change in kind. It begins with the worst. Nor is its gravity to be measured quantitatively: The intention to destroy an entire group is present in the destruction of even a small number of people from that group. It makes no sense, therefore, to speak of ending genocide later. If you end it later, you will not have ended it. If Hitler had been stopped after the murder of three million Jews, would he be said to have failed? Four hundred thousand Darfuris have already been murdered by the Janjaweed, the Arab Einsatzgruppen [Nazi paramilitary units]. If we were to prevent the murder of the 400,001st, will we be said to have succeeded?

This elementary characteristic of genocide—the requirement that the only acceptable response is an immediate and uncompromising response or else we, too, will be complicit in the crime—should have been obvious after the inhumane ditherings, the wrenchingly slow awakenings to conscience, of the '90s; but the discussion of the Darfur genocide in recent years shows that this is not at all obvious. To be sure, there is no silence about Darfur. Quite the contrary. The lamentations about Darfur are everywhere now. There is eloquence, there is protest. Unlikely coalitions are being formed. Movie stars are refusing to be muzzled, and they are standing up and being counted. Even officials and politicians feel that they must have something pained and wrathful to say. These latecomers include the president of the United States.

Hypocritical Calls for Non-U.S. Solutions

All of this is to the good, of course. In a democratic and media-maddened society, this right-thinking din is one of the conditions of political action, as domestic pressures are increasingly significant factors in the formulation of U.S. foreign policy. But it makes no sense—and, in this instance, it is a sophisticated form of indecency—to care about a problem without caring about its solution. During the Bosnia crisis, there were many people who cared about the ethnic cleansing and systematic rape of the Bosnian Muslims, but they insisted that it was a European problem with a European solution. They were half right: It was indeed a European problem, classically so. But it was perfectly plain to every honest observer of the genocide that there would be no European solution, and that the insistence upon such a solution amounted to a tender indifference to the problem.

The Darfur variety of the Bosnia hypocrisy is now upon us. We are told that this genocide must be stopped, now, now, never again, all it takes for the triumph of evil is for good men to do nothing, not on our watch, fight the power, we shall overcome—but stopped by us? Of course not. This is an African problem with an African solution. The African solution comes in two versions. There is the view that Darfur will be rescued from the genocide by the successful resolution of the negotiations taking place in Abuja—or, more precisely, that the people who are perpetrating the evil are the ones to whom we must look for the end of its perpetration. . . . This version of the African solution does not even acknowledge the requirement of military force to halt the evil. And there is the version of the African solution that looks to the troops of the African Union (AU) to do the job. [Speaker of the House] Nancy Pelosi is especially enamored of this remedy. She has boldly proclaimed that AU troops must be "given more mobility" and "freed from the restriction that limits their effectiveness," all in the name of stopping the genocide. It would be nice, wouldn't it? But, so far, the forces of the African Union

Military Force Presence Needed in Darfur

Full-scale humanitarian collapse in Darfur looms ever closer, even as the violence that will occasion this collapse relentlessly increases. Hundreds of humanitarian workers have been evacuated in recent weeks from North Darfur and eastern Chad. In turn, violence will continue to accelerate as long as the Khartoum regime succeeds in preserving the demoralized and ineffectual African Union force in Darfur as the only source of security for more than 4 million civilians, as well as the vast humanitarian operations upon which they now increasingly depend.

This is the ghastly, inescapable syllogism of genocidal destruction in Darfur. Nothing will change until a force of the sort authorized by UN Security Council Resolution 1706 (August 31, 2006) deploys to Darfur, with or without Khartoum's consent. Non-consensual deployment would be exceedingly difficult, and it certainly could not be tasked with stopping all the fighting. But such a force could provide protection to the more than 2 million displaced civilians concentrated in many scores of widely dispersed and extremely vulnerable camps—camps that have increasingly become the target of Janjaweed assaults, and that may become the target of wholesale slaughter. . . .

Eric Reeves, "Darfur: Civilian Destruction Accelerates,
International Failure Keeps Pace,"
www.sudanreeves.org, December 14, 2006.

(AU) have had no significant impact on the emergency. To ask them to do the job is to admit that you do not really need the job done.

Leave It to the Ineffective U.N.?

Then there is the other alibi for Western inaction, the distinguished one: the belief that salvation will come from blue helmets [U.N. forces]. After the slaughters of the '90s, all of which numbered the fecklessness—and even the cynicism—of the United Nations among their causes, it defies belief that people of goodwill would turn to the United Nations for effective action. The United Nations is not even prepared to call the atrocities in Darfur a genocide. Kofi Annan [U.N. Secretary-General from 1997 to 2006] says all sorts of lofty things, but everybody knows that he is only the humble servant of a notoriously recalcitrant body. Meanwhile the Sudanese regime maneuvers skillfully—what is the Chinese word for oil?—to prevent reprisals of any kind from the Security Council. And even if the United Nations were somehow to recover its ethics and its efficacy, it would take many months—in some estimates, most of a year—before a U.N. force could be deployed. No, they are not losing any sleep in Khartoum over the U.N. option.

Democrats and Republicans Impeding U.S. Involvement

There is also the view that this is an African problem with a European solution—but let us come to the heart of the matter. All these proposals for ending the genocide in Darfur are really proposals to prevent the United States from ending it. It appears that there is something even more terrible than genocide in this very terrible world, and it is the further use of American military power abroad. And in a Muslim country! Why, it would make us more unpopular. Remember that in the post-September 11, post-Operation Iraqi Freedom environment, the sensitivities of Muslims—insofar as they can be clearly known and accurately predicted—must not be further offended. Never mind that they themselves give gross offense: This is a genocide committed by Muslims against Muslims that no Muslims are racing to stop. The poor Darfuris: Their plight interferes with the anti-imperialist integrity of liberals in the only country in the world with the power and the authority (yes, still) to help them. The Democrats in Washington are now clamoring for the appointment of a special envoy to Sudan. That is to say, they are searching for reasons to deflect the responsibility of refusing to let crimes against humanity stand. In the matter of genocide, the party of [former president Bill] Clinton is still the party of Clinton.

But it is not only, or mainly, the Democrats who impede a U.S.—or a U.S.-led, or a U.S.-NATO—campaign against the killers. This is a Republican era, after all. And the record of the [George W.] Bush administration on Darfur has been disgraceful. President Bush has his own uses for all the alibis. He is not inclined to order one more American soldier into action. (But would the camels of the Janjaweed pose a tactical challenge to us? Surely all that is required is a little shock and no awe at all.) And there are other disturbing reasons for Bush's tepidity about Darfur. One of them, again, is Sudan's oil, which suddenly confers upon this repulsive state a certain strategic prestige. And there is also the haunting memory of Sudan's previous hospitality to anti-American jihadist terrorism. In the view of the White House, then, an intervention in Darfur may be counter to American interests. So, in this crisis, too, the streets of Washington now run with realism.

Why Not the United States?

All this is grotesque. Sure, interventions are always more complicated than planned (though they are rarely as poorly planned as Iraq, which must not serve as the only model); but not all interventions are quagmires waiting to happen. And the risks to American values if we fail to act against genocide are far greater than the risks to American interests if we act against it. Is Iraq now all that the United States needs to know? Will we allow Abu Ghraib and Guantánamo Bay [sites of prisoner abuse by U.S. forces] to disqualify us from our moral and historical role in the world? Is idealism in U.S. foreign policy only for fair weather? What is so unconscionable about nation-building anyway? Why will we never get the question of genocide right, when, in some ways, it is the easiest question of all? The discussion of Darfur, even by many people whose outrage is sincere, has become a festival of bad faith. Everybody wants to do everything but what must be done. It is the season of heartless bleeding hearts.

> *"From a realistic point of view, there is nothing U.S. military intervention can accomplish in [Darfur] Sudan except to make things far worse."*

The United States Should Not Intervene in Darfur

Justin Raimondo

In this viewpoint, Justin Raimondo argues that U.S. military intervention in Darfur will make the situation there worse and could precipitate terrorist attacks on the United States. Raimondo thinks that everyone, neoconservatives (neocons) and liberals alike, have hidden agendas when it comes to calling for aid to Darfur. He thinks the United States should privately send humanitarian aid to Darfur, but not U.S. troops. Justin Raimondo is the editorial director of Antiwar.com, a program of the Randolph Bourne Institute that promotes a noninterventionist policy for the United States.

As you read, consider the following questions:

1. Which countries suffered genocides in the 1990s?
2. How long would it take before a United Nations force could be deployed in Darfur?

Justin Raimondo, "What About Darfur? The Case Against Intervention," *www.antiwar.com*, May 1, 2006. Reproduced by permission.

3. According to Raimondo, what are the reasons that
President Bush has been "tepid" about Darfur?

Whenever I speak on campus, I always get the "But what
about Darfur?" question. This usually comes in tandem
with the inevitable Holocaust question, which goes something
like this: "Yes, I agree with your opposition to the Iraq war,
and your anti-interventionist sentiments in general, but what
about our moral responsibility to prevent another Holocaust?"
This is usually accompanied by a paean to "the good war," i.e.,
World War II, and the assertion that "of course" we had to intervene (and not just because of Pearl Harbor).

I will spare the reader my detailed answer to enthusiasts of
"the good war," except to say that if we hadn't intervened in
World War II at precisely the moment Hitler turned on Stalin,
the likelihood of the two totalitarian monsters destroying each
other is a bit more than mere speculation. I will also note that
the Holocaust, far from being prevented by World War II, was
instead hastened and accelerated by the conflict. American intervention in the European war had nothing to do with the
Holocaust, did nothing to prevent it, and may have worsened
it.

Darfur Is the Cause Célèbre

In any case, to get back to the case of Darfur: my questioner, I
should point out, is usually not some warmongering neocon
[neoconservative], but the most well-meaning of all lefties,
who is savagely critical of the neoconservative agenda of "de-
mocratizing" the Middle East at gunpoint, but, when it comes
to Darfur, all discernment, all the lessons of the past, are
thrown out the window, and emotions take over. It is like an
alcoholic, who, after a long abstinence, quaffs a bit of wine, or
has half a beer: after just a little sip, all caution is abandoned,
and they find him the next day, passed out in the street.

Darfur, where as many as 300,000 may have been killed,
has become an international cause célèbre and rallying cry for

the internationalist liberals, the kind who pride themselves on having a conscience and who constantly invoke the tragedy of Darfur as a potential model for "humanitarian intervention." They think that they are different from the neocons in kind because they advocate intervention for a "good" cause, because they are motivated by kindness, benevolence, and all those other liberal internationalist virtues that make them such so much better people than [neoconservatives] Richard Perle [a fellow at the conservative think tank American Enterprise Institute] and Bill Kristol [the editor of *Weekly Standard*].

Well-Worn Pattern

This shows that whatever foreign policy debate occurs in this country is not about the policy—almost no one questions the wisdom and absolute necessity of global interventionism—but about motivation: President [George W.] Bush, [Secretary of Defense 2001–2006] Donald Rumsfeld, and Condi Rice [Secretary of State under Bush] care about oil, money, Israel, and self-glorification, not necessarily in that order. We care about helping poor blacks, stopping genocide, and dispensing American treasure to the underprivileged albeit deserving peoples of the Third World.

To get a little perspective on this, let's look at what the invaluable John Laughland, a writer and longtime observer of the War Party, has to say:

> The Darfur crisis is following a pattern which is so well-worn now that it has almost become routine. Saturation reporting from a crisis region; emergency calls for help broadcast on the electronic media (such as the one recently on the BBC Radio 4 flagship "Today" programme); televised pictures of refugees; lurid stories of "mass rapes," which are surely designed to titillate as much to provoke outrage; reproachful evocations of the Rwandan genocide; demands that something must be done ("How can we stand idly by?", etc.); editorials in the *Daily Telegraph* calling for a return to

the days of Rudyard Kipling's benevolent imperialism; and, finally, the announcement that plans are indeed being drawn up for an intervention.

Writing in 2004, Laughland averred that Western intervention is "inevitable," and it looks like he was right on the money. *The Washington Post* carried a story, prominently featured in the Sunday edition, about the "growing outcry" to "do something" about Sudan:

"Massive 'Stop Genocide' rallies are planned on the Mall and across the nation today to urge the Bush administration to take stronger action to end the violence in Sudan's Darfur region. Thousands of people are expected to converge on Washington, including 240 busloads of activists from 41 states, local and national politicians and such celebrity speakers as actor George Clooney, Holocaust survivor and author Elie Wiesel, and Olympic speed skater Joey Cheek."

While early reports of plans for the demonstration reported an expected turnout of 100,000-plus, the rally permit obtained by the "Save Darfur Coalition" estimated 10,000–15,000, and the actual numbers were far less. Reuters generously reported "several thousands," but, never mind that: the sparse numbers were magnified by the star power of the celebrity speakers. Piggybacking on titans of Hollywood and the world of sports like Clooney and Cheek, Democratic party bigwigs—including Sen. Barack Obama, D-Ill., and House Democratic leader Nancy Pelosi of California—sought to extract political benefits from this supposedly spontaneous upsurge of interventionist sentiment.

That, only a few days before, Osama bin Laden had made Sudan the focus of another of his tirades against the West—warning the Muslim world that Darfur would be the next entry point for the "Crusader-Zionists"—was surely a coincidence, albeit an enormously convenient one for the motley collection of liberal do-gooders, Hollywood glamour-pusses, and Christian zealots who make up the "Save Darfur Coali-

Cartoon by Signe Wilkinson, "Never Again," photograph. Signe Wilkinson Editorial Cartoon © 2004 Signe Wilkinson. Used with the permission of Signe Wilkinson and the Washington Post Writers Group in conjunction with the Cartoonist Group.

tion." President Bush was glad to endorse the rally: "For those of you who are going out to march for justice, you represent the best of our country," Bush said at a meeting with persons described as "Darfur advocates" in news reports.

The War Party

Before we send tens of thousands more American troops into a very troubled region of the world, let us examine what these "Darfur advocates" are advocating. Both Tony Blair [British prime minister] and retired U.S. general Wesley Clark have argued in favor of intervention, raising the "successful" war and occupation in Kosovo as a model. That was one war we didn't hear much about from the great mass of present-day "anti-war" protesters, who apparently thought that attacking a country that represented no threat to the U.S. and had never attacked us was okay, so long as it was done by a Democratic president. By going into Darfur under the rubric of "humanitarianism," the War Party can sell to anti-Bush liberals the idea of opening up another front in the Muslim world.

The Dubai brouhaha showed how easily anti-Arab sentiment can be exploited on the ostensible "Left" and utilized by the War Party to demonstrate their effective control of both major political parties—and distance themselves from an increasingly unpopular administration. The Darfur campaign is another example of their strategic shift: in both instances, instead of following President Bush's lead, they stood in opposition to the White House. Up until this point, the Bush team has been skeptical of getting involved in Sudan. As the Bush White House drags its feet in provoking the Iranians into war, the War Party is turning increasingly to the Democrats—and the ostensible liberal-Left—for support. This is beginning to pay off, as [Senator, Democratic presidential candidate, and former first lady] Hillary Clinton tries to out-hawk the GOP [Republican Party] on the Iranian nukes issue, and leading Democrats take up the banner of Darfur.

U.S. Military Intervention Will Make Things Worse

From a realistic point of view, there is nothing U.S. military intervention can accomplish in Sudan except to make things far worse. Sudan would soon become Iraq II, with an influx of jihadists and a nationalistic reaction against what would become, after a short time, a de facto occupation very similar to what the Iraqis have to endure. The rebel groups, aided by Sudan's neighbors, such as Ethiopia and Eritrea, would metastasize, more weapons would pour into the region, and the probable result would be a humanitarian disaster on a much larger scale. Intervention, in short, would lead to the exact opposite of its intended result—a principle that, as a libertarian, I hold is true in economics as well as foreign policy.

But you don't have to be a libertarian to see the folly of interventionism in the case of Darfur, or Iraq. In the latter, it is the presence of the U.S. occupation force that empowers the rising anti-U.S. insurgency: the same principle would operate in Sudan. There is no reason to believe that we would be welcomed with open arms by the Sudanese any more than we were by the Iraqis. An initial euphoria—some of it staged—would soon be supplanted by a growing resentment, and the influx of jihadists would destabilize the entire region, requiring increased U.S. and "allied" forces.

"Saving" Darfur would mean opening up another theater in what the neocons refer to as "World War IV." Spreading outward from Iraq, this global conflict will pit the U.S. against a wide variety of enemies, both freelance and state-sponsored, swelling the ranks of terrorist outfits and inviting further attacks on U.S. soil. This could be construed as a "humanitarian" intervention only in the Bizarro World inhabited by our leaders, including those hailing from the entertainment industry.

A coalition of liberal internationalists, opportunistic politicians of both parties, and the usual neocon suspects have banded together to lure us into yet another quagmire, this one in Africa. This new crusade is so imbued with the aura of humanitarian uplift that anyone who questions the wisdom of intervening in a complicated and obscure civil war will be denounced as a "racist" who doesn't give a hoot about Africa.

Help by Minding Own Business

Oh, so you're against intervening in Darfur, eh? Don't you care about starving African babies? That our intervention will likely as not lead to more starving African babies, rather than less, is in my opinion indubitably true, yet even if it were not, intervention would still be a mistake. It would be a grave error because there is no lack of "humanitarian disasters" in this world, and the alleviation of all of them cannot be the goal of U.S. foreign policy. That would have to mean perpetual warfare, on a global scale, waged by the U.S. against countless legions of enemies, including many yet to be born.

It is a recipe for endless trouble, increasing expenditures, and eventual bankruptcy, moral as well as financial. Because, in the end, we'll discover that the whole thing was cooked up by disparate interests with hidden agendas, in order to profit financially or politically. The truth will come out: it always does.

We cannot help Africa, except by trading with it and increasing our humanitarian private efforts to alleviate suffering. The least we can do, however, is to stop encouraging the worst, most illiberal elements by subsidizing governments like those of Ethiopia and Eritrea, run by common thugs paid to do America's bidding. If we really want to help Africa, we'll stay out of their internal political affairs, start granting more visas from that continent, and get over our own sense of moral superiority that lets us imagine we can somehow uplift the entire world to the level of a typical American suburb.

Finally, if this doesn't underscore the unselfconscious irrationality of the "left"-wing do-gooder-Hollywood wing of the War Party, then nothing does.

> *"It is an embarrassing tragedy to see a departure from our nation's historic leadership as a champion of human rights."*

The United States Should Not Practice Torture Even to Win the War on Terrorism

Jimmy Carter

In the following viewpoint, former U.S. President Jimmy Carter asserts that U.S. antiterrorist policies that allow and condone prisoner abuse and torture are immoral and are eroding human rights around the world. Carter says changes to U.S. policy since 9/11 have damaged the country's reputation and led the country away from its founding principles and its role as a protector of human rights. Jimmy Carter, the thirty-ninth U.S. president, is the founder of the Carter Center, which seeks to promote human rights.

As you read, consider the following questions:

1. Approximately how many people have been incarcerated at Guantanamo, Cuba?

2. According to the Red Cross, what percent of the prisoners held at Abu Ghraib are there by mistake?

3. What is determined at a CSRT?

4. What is the primary goal of torture?

This is an especially unpleasant [viewpoint] to write, because it includes some embarrassing assessments of the government I have led and whose values I have defended. The concept that America maintains superior moral and ethical standards propelled us, immediately after the 9/11 attacks, into a global leadership role in combating terrorism. Our nation had long raised the banner of human rights for all others to see and follow, a role that has been described as a "self-assigned Messianic role in world affairs." To restore and then maintain these national values, it is important that Americans understand the revolutionary changes in policy that we are using to reach our crucial goal of self-protection.

A Legacy of Rights

I grew up in the Deep South, in a region where slavery had been a dominant factor of life for almost 250 years until abolished by ratification of the Fourteenth and Fifteenth Amendments to the U.S. Constitution in 1868 and 1870. During my boyhood, however, slavery had been replaced by racial segregation based on the U.S. Supreme Court's 1896 ruling that "separate but equal" treatment of black people was both legal and acceptable. With the political courage of President Harry Truman, the legal discrimination was eliminated in the U.S. armed forces in 1948, including the submarine in which I was serving, and then throughout our nation within the next two decades by the civil rights movement headed by Martin Luther King Jr. and the strong leadership of President Lyndon Johnson.

This triumph of civil rights at home did not preclude America's acceptance and support of some of the most brutal foreign regimes in our hemisphere and other regions, which blatantly violated the human rights of their own citizens. As a newly elected president, I announced that the protection of these rights would be the foundation of our country's foreign policy, and I persistently took action to implement this commitment. It has been gratifying to observe a wave of democratization sweep across our hemisphere and in other regions, as the fundamental rights of freedom were respected.

Post 9/11 Changes

During the past four years there have been dramatic changes in our nation's policies toward protecting these rights. Many of our citizens have accepted these unprecedented policies because of the fear of terrorist attacks, but the damage to America's reputation has been extensive. Formerly admired almost universally as the preeminent champion of human rights, the United States now has become one of the foremost targets of respected international organizations concerned about these basic principles of democratic life. Some of our actions are similar to those of abusive regimes that we have historically condemned.

Following the attacks of 9/11, the U.S. government overreacted by detaining more than twelve hundred innocent men throughout America, none of whom were ever convicted of any crime related to terrorism. Their identities have been kept secret, and they were never given the right to hear charges against themselves or to have legal counsel. Almost all of them were Arabs or Muslims, and many have been forced to leave America. . . .

Guantánamo

A large number of men and some young boys have been captured in the wars in Afghanistan and Iraq and transferred to an American prison camp in Guantánamo, Cuba, where about 520 people from forty nations have been incarcerated and held incommunicado for more than three years, almost all without legal counsel and with no charges leveled against them. It has also been confirmed by U.S. officials that many have been physically abused.

After visiting six of the twenty-five or so U.S. prisons, the International Committee of the Red Cross reported registering 107 detainees under eighteen, some as young as eight years old. The journalist Seymour Hersh reported in May 2005 that Defense Secretary Donald Rumsfeld had received a report that there were "800–900 Pakistani boys 13–15 years of age in custody." The International Red Cross, Amnesty International, and the Pentagon have gathered substantial testimony of torture of children, confirmed by soldiers who witnessed or participated in the abuse. In addition to personal testimony from children about physical and mental mistreatment, a report from Brigadier General Janis Karpinski, formerly in charge of Abu Ghraib [another camp where prisoner abuse by U.S. military occurred], described a visit to an eleven-year-old detainee in the cell block that housed high-risk prisoners. The general recalled that the child was weeping, and "he told me he was almost twelve," and that "he really wanted to see his mother, could he please call his mother." Children like this eleven-year-old have been denied the right to see their parents, a lawyer, or anyone else, and were not told why they were detained. A Pentagon spokesman told Mr. Hersh that "age is not a determining factor in detention."

Physicians for Human Rights reported in April 2005 that "at least since 2002, the United States has been engaged in systematic psychological torture" of Guantánamo detainees that has "led to devastating health consequences for the individuals subjected to" it. The prisoners' outlook on life was not improved when the Secretary of Defense declared that most of them would not be released even if they were someday tried and found to be innocent.

Dr. Burton J. Lee III, President George H. W. Bush's personal White House physician, issued this statement:

"Reports of torture by U.S. forces have been accompanied by evidence that military medical personnel have played a role in this abuse and by new military ethical guidelines that in effect authorize complicity by health professionals in ill-treatment of detainees. These new guidelines distort traditional ethical rules beyond recognition to serve the interests of interrogators, not doctors and detainees. . . . Systematic torture, sanctioned by the government and aided and abetted by our own profession, is not acceptable. As health professionals, we should support the growing calls for an independent, bipartisan commission to investigate torture in Iraq, Afghanistan, Guantánamo Bay and elsewhere, and demand restoration of ethical standards that protect physicians, nurses, medics and psychologists from becoming facilitators of abuse. America cannot continue down this road. Torture demonstrates weakness, not strength. It does not show understanding, power or magnanimity. It is not leadership. It is a reaction of government officials overwhelmed by fear who succumb to conduct unworthy of them and of the citizens of the United States."

Widespread Prisoner Abuse

The terrible pictures from Abu Ghraib prison in Iraq have brought discredit on our country. This is especially disturbing, since U.S. intelligence officers estimated to the Red Cross that 70 to 90 percent of the detainees at this prison were held by mistake. Military officials reported that at least 108 prisoners have died in American custody in Iraq, Afghanistan, and other secret locations just since 2002, with homicide acknowledged as the cause of death in at least 28 cases. The fact that only one of these was in Abu Ghraib prison indicates the widespread pattern of prisoner abuse, certainly not limited to the actions or decisions of just a few rogue enlisted persons.

Iraqi major general Abed Hamed Mowhoush reported voluntarily to American officials in Baghdad in an attempt to locate his sons, and was detained, tortured, and stuffed inside a green sleeping bag, where he died from trauma and suffocation on November 26, 2003.

The superficial investigations under the auspices of the Department of Defense have made it obvious that no high-level military officers or government officials will be held accountable, but there is no doubt that their public statements and private directives cast doubt and sometimes ridicule on the applicability of international standards of human rights and the treatment of prisoners.

Lowered Standards

In November 2003 and again in June 2005, deeply concerned about the adverse impact of these new U.S. policies in other nations, The Carter Center hosted leading defenders of human rights and democracy movements from several dozen countries. My cochairs at both conferences were the U.N. High Commissioners for Human Rights, and other international human rights organizations played a key role in the discussions.

What we learned in these sessions was quite disturbing, the reports coming from courageous and effective nonviolent activists who take great risks in dangerous circumstances to protect freedom and the rights of others. Many of them had been either imprisoned or severely harassed as a result of holding their governments accountable to international standards of human rights and the principles of democracy. They were convinced that there had been a high-level, broad-based, and deliberate change in U.S. policy, abandoning or lowering our long-standing commitment to protect fundamental human rights within our nation and throughout the world. The human rights defenders also reported in 2003 that a large number of accused persons were being sent from America to

The McCain Amendment to Prohibit Cruel, Inhuman, and Degrading Treatment of Prisoners

"Mr. President, I rise to offer an amendment that would (1) establish the Army Field Manual as the uniform standard for the interrogation of Department of Defense detainees and (2) prohibit cruel, inhuman, and degrading treatment of persons in the detention of the U.S. government....

Mr. President, to fight terrorism we need intelligence. That much is obvious. What should also be obvious is that the intelligence we collect must be reliable and acquired humanely, under clear standards understood by all our fighting men and women. To do differently not only offends our values as Americans, but undermines our war effort, because abuse of prisoners harms—not helps—us in the war on terror. First, subjecting prisoners to abuse leads to bad intelligence, because under torture a detainee will tell his interrogator anything to make the pain stop. Second, mistreatment of our prisoners endangers U.S. troops who might be captured by the enemy - if not in this war, then in the next. And third, prisoner abuses exact on us a terrible toll in the war of ideas, because inevitably these abuses become public. When they do, the cruel actions of a few darken the reputation of our country in the eyes of millions. American values should win against all others in any war of ideas, and we can't let prisoner abuse tarnish our image.

John McCain, "Statement of Senator John McCain Statement on Detainee Amendments on (1) the Army Field Manual and (2) Cruel, Inhumane, Degrading Treatment," November 4, 2005, http://mccain.senate.gov.

selected foreign countries where torture was acceptable as a means of extracting information. This allegation was strongly denied by officials who represented the U.S. government at this conference.

U.S. Policies Eroding Human Rights Abroad

The participants were in broad agreement that recent policies of the United States were being adopted and distorted by opportunistic regimes to serve their own interests. They told of a general retreat by their governments from previous human rights commitments, and emphasized that there was a danger of setting back democratic movements by decades in some of their countries. Participants explained that oppressive leaders had been emboldened to persecute and silence outspoken citizens under the guise of fighting terrorism, and that this excuse was deflecting pressure coming from the United States and other powers regarding human rights violations. The consequence was that many lawyers, professors, doctors, and journalists had been labeled terrorists, often for merely criticizing a particular policy or for carrying out their daily work. We heard about many cases involving human rights attorneys being charged with abetting terrorists simply for defending accused persons.

Equally disturbing were reports that the United States government is in some cases contributing directly to an erosion of human rights protection by encouraging governments to adopt regressive counterterrorism policies that lead to the undermining of democratic principles and the rule of law, often going far beyond the U.S. Patriot Act.

We all were encouraged because the most onerous of the new U.S. policies were being questioned in the Congress and through the federal court system and would ultimately be corrected. Although many legal issues had not yet reached the final appellate level to be clarified, most contested domestic cases had been resolved favorably, and the United States Supreme Court ruled in June 2004 that U.S. federal courts "have jurisdiction to consider challenges to the legality of the detentions of foreign nationals captured abroad in connection with hostilities and incarcerated at Guantánamo Bay."

While none of the Guantánamo detainees has yet obtained such a review because of government intransigence, a small number of them have been visited by lawyers seeking to file *habeas corpus* appeals. The U.S. administration has minimized compliance with the Supreme Court decision by establishing combatant status review tribunals (CSRT) to determine if a detainee is an "enemy combatant." Each CSRT is a panel of three military officers, ostensibly relying on secret evidence, to determine if the label "enemy combatant" should remain attached to each detainee, who still has no access to legal counsel to assist him. It took two and a half years after the detainees arrived there, but the decision was the first step toward forcing the administration to restore the rule of law in our dealings with foreigners in American custody.

In most of the countries represented at our human rights conferences, including young democracies, such checks and balances in the judicial system are not so well developed and make the questioning and reversal of abusive policies much less likely.

Another subject of concern among those who came from Northern Ireland, Turkey, Burma, Colombia, Israel, the occupied Palestinian territories, Uzbekistan, and other conflict-ridden societies was that the early use of military force and an announced policy of preemptive war sent a signal that violence had become a much more acceptable alternative to peaceful negotiations in the resolution of differences. The general consensus of these experts on democracy and freedom was that policies based on violence always result in a cycle of escalated violence.

Prisoner Vulnerability

It is apparent that prisoners of war are among the most vulnerable of people. Not only are they completely under the control of their captors, but in a time of conflict, the hatred and brutality of the battlefield are very likely to be mirrored within military prison walls. Other well-known factors are that wartime secrecy often cloaks the orders and policies of superiors and the actions of subordinates, and some elements of national hatred and fear are elevated by the psychology of war.

My own family experienced the impact of these factors when my favorite uncle, navy petty officer Tom Gordy, was brutally treated as a prisoner of war after being captured in Guam by the Japanese within a month of the attack on Pearl Harbor in 1941. After two years he was reported to be dead but was found after Japan's surrender, weighing eighty-five pounds, debilitated by four years of physical and psychological mistreatment.

Geneva Conventions

The prevalence of such abuse of captured servicemen and -women during World War II induced the community of nations to come together to define quite precisely the basic guarantees of proper treatment for prisoners. These restraints are the result of an international conference held in Geneva, Switzerland, in 1949, and redefined and expanded what are known as the "Geneva Conventions." The authenticity and universal applicability of these guarantees were never questioned by a democratic power—until recently, and by America! Instead of honoring the historic restraints, our political leaders decided to violate them, using the excuse that we are at war against terrorism. It is obvious that the Geneva Conventions were designed specifically to protect prisoners of war, not prisoners of peace. . . .

Extraordinary Rendition: Extraordinary Torture

Subsequent evidence revealed that despite previous denials at our first human rights conference, American leaders had adopted a supplementary policy of transferring prisoners to foreign countries, including Egypt, Saudi Arabia, Syria, Morocco, Jordan, and Uzbekistan, most of which have been condemned in our government's annual human rights reports for habitually using torture to extract information. Although opposed by the State Department, this practice has been approved at the top levels of U.S. government. It is known as "extraordinary rendition," and the official excuses are that the victims have been classified as "illegal enemy combatants" and that our military or CIA personnel "don't know for certain" that they will be tortured. Members of Congress and legal specialists estimate that 150 prisoners have been included in this exceptional program. The techniques of torture are almost indescribably terrible, including, as a U.S. ambassador to one of the recipient countries reported, "partial boiling of a hand or an arm," with at least two prisoners boiled to death.

Of the many cases, one of the few that has been publicized involves the capture of a Canadian citizen, Maher Arar, when he was changing planes at Kennedy Airport in New York. He was shackled, loaded by U.S. agents into a Gulfstream 5 corporate jet, and taken to Syria, where he was abused for a year before being released after no evidence was found against him. U.S. officials knew what was happening. As the State Department had stated earlier about human rights abuses in Syria, "Former prisoners and detainees have reported that torture methods include electrical shocks, pulling out fingernails, the forced insertion of objects into the rectum, beatings, sometimes while the victim is suspended from the ceiling, hyperextension of the spine, and the use of a chair that bends backwards to asphyxiate the victim or fracture the spine."

Aside from the humanitarian aspects, it is well known that, under excruciating torture, a prisoner will admit almost any suggested crime. Such confessions are, of course, not admissible in trials in civilized nations. The primary goal of torture or the threat of torture is not to obtain convictions for crimes, but to engender and maintain fear. Some of our leaders have found that it is easy to forgo human rights for those who are considered to be subhuman, or "enemy combatants.". . .

One serious consequence of this abominable procedure is the question of what to do with the tortured prisoners when they are proven innocent. Can they be released and free to give public testimony against the United States of America or even file lawsuits against our country, as a few of them have already done? Even if held in prison, some of them have become special problems because high-profile terrorists who were actually involved in the 9/11 attack have asked for them to be witnesses. Trials of these known criminals have been held in abeyance because we cannot afford to let the former or still-incarcerated detainees testify.

Instead of our correcting the basic problem, more and more prisoners are being retained, and there is less access to the facts about their treatment. A report released in March 2005 by Human Rights First said that the number of detainees in U.S. custody in Iraq and Afghanistan has grown, just during the preceding six months, from six thousand to more than eleven thousand, and that the level of secrecy surrounding American detention operations has intensified. . . .

Return to Our Founding Principles

As our nation was being founded, George Washington decided to establish in America an innovative "policy of humanity." In 2003 I wrote a novel about our Revolutionary War, after six years of study and research. One of my most shocking discoveries was that British officers often ordered that "no quarter be granted" to Americans who surrendered on the battlefield. They were to be summarily executed. A vivid example of this was in the battle of Briar Creek, in northeast Georgia, when this order was given along with clear instructions that any British soldier who took a prisoner alive would be deprived of his rum ration for a month. General Washington condemned the practice and announced a more enlightened approach to warfare. Even though some American revolutionaries were later guilty of the same brutality, they were in violation of absolutely clear directives from their top commander.

It is an embarrassing tragedy to see a departure from our nation's historic leadership as a champion of human rights, with the abandonment defended legally by top officials. Only the American people can redirect our government's legal, religious, and political commitments to these ancient and unchanging moral principles.

> "The argument is not whether torture is
> ever permissible, but when."

The United States
Should Practice Torture Under
Some Circumstances

Charles Krauthamer

In this viewpoint, Charles Krauthammer says there are times when torture is necessary. Krauthammer acknowledges that torture is a "monstrous evil." But, he says there are instances when torture should be used to save the lives of soldiers and countrymen. Leaders who fail to use torture to gain information that has potential to save lives are morally wrong says Krauthammer. Charles Krauthammer is a Pulitzer Prize–winning columnist and commentator.

As you read, consider the following questions:

1. Why are ordinary soldier prisoners perhaps entitled to more privileges than domestic prisoners? To what are ordinary soldier prisoners entitled?

2. What are the two contingencies where Krauthammer would allow torture?

3. Did the Israelis follow the 1987 Landau Commission when they interrogated the driver of the car used in the Waxman kidnapping?

Let's begin with a few analytic distinctions. For the purpose of torture and prisoner maltreatment, there are three kinds of war prisoners:

Ordinary Soldier

First, there is the ordinary soldier caught on the field of battle. There is no question that he is entitled to humane treatment. Indeed, we have no right to disturb a hair on his head. His detention has but a single purpose: to keep him *hors de combat* [out of the fight]. The proof of that proposition is that if there were a better way to keep him off the battlefield that did not require his detention, we would let him go. Indeed, during one year of the Civil War, the two sides did try an alternative. They mutually "paroled" captured enemy soldiers, i.e., released them to return home on the pledge that they would not take up arms again. (The experiment failed for a foreseeable reason: cheating. [General Ulysses S.] Grant found that some paroled Confederates had reenlisted.)

Because the only purpose of detention in these circumstances is to prevent the prisoner from becoming a combatant again, he is entitled to all the protections and dignity of an ordinary domestic prisoner—indeed, more privileges, because, unlike the domestic prisoner, he has committed no crime. He merely had the misfortune to enlist on the other side of a legitimate war. He is therefore entitled to many of the privileges enjoyed by an ordinary citizen—the right to send correspondence, to engage in athletic activity and intellectual pursuits, to receive allowances from relatives—except, of course, for the freedom to leave the prison.

Captured Terrorist

Second, there is the captured terrorist. A terrorist is by profession, indeed by definition, an unlawful combatant: He lives outside the laws of war because he does not wear a uniform, he hides among civilians, and he deliberately targets innocents. He is entitled to no protections whatsoever. People seem to think that the postwar Geneva Conventions were written only to protect detainees. In fact, their deeper purpose was to provide a deterrent to the kind of barbaric treatment of civilians that had become so horribly apparent during the first half of the 20th century, and in particular, during the Second World War. The idea was to deter the abuse of civilians by promising combatants who treated noncombatants well that they themselves would be treated according to a code of dignity if captured—and, crucially, that they would be denied the protections of that code if they broke the laws of war and abused civilians themselves.

Breaking the laws of war and abusing civilians are what, to understate the matter vastly, terrorists do for a living. They are entitled, therefore, to nothing. Anyone who blows up a car bomb in a market deserves to spend the rest of his life roasting on a spit over an open fire. But we don't do that because we do not descend to the level of our enemy. We don't do that because, unlike him, we are civilized. Even though terrorists are entitled to no humane treatment, we give it to them because it is in our nature as a moral and humane people. And when on rare occasions we fail to do that, as has occurred in several of the fronts of the war on terror, we are duly disgraced.

The norm, however, is how the majority of prisoners at Guantanamo have been treated. We give them three meals a day, superior medical care, and provision to pray five times a day. Our scrupulousness extends even to providing them with their own Korans [Muslim holy book], which is the only reason alleged abuses of the Koran at Guantanamo ever became an issue. That we should have provided those who kill innocents in the name of Islam with precisely the document that inspires their barbarism is a sign of the absurd lengths to which we often go in extending undeserved humanity to terrorist prisoners.

Terrorist with Information

Third, there is the terrorist with information. Here the issue of torture gets complicated and the easy pieties don't so easily apply. Let's take the textbook case. Ethics 101: A terrorist has planted a nuclear bomb in New York City. It will go off in one hour. A million people will die. You capture the terrorist. He knows where it is. He's not talking.

Question: If you have the slightest belief that hanging this man by his thumbs will get you the information to save a million people, are you permitted to do it?

Now, on most issues regarding torture, I confess tentativeness and uncertainty. But on this issue, there can be no uncertainty: Not only is it permissible to hang this miscreant by his thumbs. It is a moral duty.

Yes, you say, but that's an extreme and very hypothetical case. Well, not as hypothetical as you think. Sure, the (nuclear) scale is hypothetical, but in the age of the car- and suicide-bomber, terrorists are often captured who have just set a car bomb to go off or sent a suicide bomber out to a coffee shop, and you only have minutes to find out where the attack is to take place. This "hypothetical" is common enough that the Israelis have a term for precisely that situation: the ticking time bomb problem.

Not *Whether*, but *When*

And even if the example I gave were entirely hypothetical, the conclusion—yes, in this case even torture is permissible—is telling because it establishes the principle: Torture is not always impermissible. However rare the cases, there are circumstances in which, by any rational moral calculus, torture not only would be permissible but would be required (to acquire life-saving information). And once you've established the principle, to paraphrase George Bernard Shaw, all that's left to haggle about is the price. In the case of torture, that means that the argument is not *whether* torture is ever permissible, but *when*—i.e., under what obviously stringent circumstances: how big, how imminent, how preventable the ticking time bomb.

That is why the [Senator John] McCain amendment [amends the Army Field Manual to ban cruel, inhuman, or degrading treatment of any prisoner], which by mandating "torture never" refuses even to recognize the legitimacy of any moral calculus, cannot be right. There must be exceptions. The real argument should be over what constitutes a legitimate exception.

Let's take an example that is far from hypothetical. You capture Khalid Sheikh Mohammed in Pakistan. He not only has already killed innocents, he is deeply involved in the planning for the present and future killing of innocents. He not only was the architect of the 9/11 attack that killed nearly three thousand people in one day, most of them dying a terrible, agonizing, indeed tortured death. But as the top al Qaeda planner and logistical expert he also knows a lot about terror attacks to come. He knows plans, identities, contacts, materials, cell locations, safe houses, cased targets, etc. What do you do with him?

Black Sites

We have recently learned that since 9/11 the United States has maintained a series of "black sites" around the world, secret detention centers where presumably high-level terrorists like Khalid Sheikh Mohammed have been imprisoned. The world is scandalized. Black sites? Secret detention? [Former President] Jimmy Carter calls this "a profound and radical change

Why We Need Torture

Isolated, confused, weary, hungry, frightened, and tormented, Sheikh Mohammed [considered a top architect of the World Trade Center bombings] would gradually be reduced to a seething collection of simple needs, all of them controlled by his interrogators.

The key to filling all those needs would be the same: *to talk.*

We hear a lot these days about America's overpowering military technology; about the professionalism of its warriors; about the sophistication of its weaponry, eavesdropping, and telemetry; but right now the most vital weapon in its arsenal may well be the art of interrogation. To counter an enemy who relies on stealth and surprise, the most valuable tool is information, and often the only source of that information is the enemy himself. Men like Sheikh Mohammed who have been taken alive in this war are classic candidates for the most cunning practices of this dark art. Intellectual, sophisticated, deeply religious, and well trained, they present a perfect challenge for the interrogator. Getting at the information they possess could allow us to thwart major attacks, unravel their organization, and save thousands of lives. They and their situation pose one of the strongest arguments in modern times for the use of torture.

Mark Bowden, "The Dark Art of Interrogation,"
Atlantic Monthly, *October 2003.*

in the ... moral values of our country." The Council of Europe demands an investigation, calling the claims "extremely worrying." Its human rights commissioner declares "such practices" to constitute "a serious human rights violation, and further proof of the crisis of values" that has engulfed the war on terror. The gnashing of teeth and rending of garments has been considerable.

I myself have not gnashed a single tooth. My garments remain entirely unrent. Indeed, I feel reassured. It would be a gross dereliction of duty for any government *not* to keep Khalid Sheikh Mohammed isolated, disoriented, alone, despairing, cold and sleepless, in some godforsaken hidden location in order to find out what he knew about plans for future mass murder. What are we supposed to do? Give him a nice cell in a warm Manhattan prison, complete with Miranda rights, a mellifluent lawyer, and his own website? Are not those the kinds of courtesies we extended to the 1993 World Trade Center bombers, then congratulated ourselves on how we "brought to justice" those responsible for an attack that barely failed to kill tens of thousands of Americans, only to discover a decade later that we had accomplished nothing—indeed, that some of the disclosures at the trial had helped Osama bin Laden avoid U.S. surveillance?

Have we learned nothing from 9/11? Are we prepared to go back with complete amnesia to the domestic-crime model of dealing with terrorists, which allowed us to sleepwalk through the nineties while al Qaeda incubated and grew and metastasized unmolested until on 9/11 it finished what the first World Trade Center bombers had begun?

Obligation to Do What Is Neccesary

Let's assume (and hope) that Khalid Sheikh Mohammed has been kept in one of these black sites, say, a cell somewhere in Romania, held entirely incommunicado and subjected to the kind of "coercive interrogation" that I described above. . . .

Consider, for example, injection with sodium pentathol. (Colloquially known as "truth serum," it is nothing of the sort. It is a barbiturate whose purpose is to sedate. Its effects are much like that of alcohol: disinhibiting the higher brain centers to make someone more likely to disclose information or thoughts that might otherwise be guarded.) Forcible sedation is a clear violation of bodily integrity. In a civilian context it would be considered assault. It is certainly impermissible under any prohibition of cruel, inhuman, or degrading treatment.

Let's posit that during the interrogation of Khalid Sheikh Mohammed, perhaps early on, we got intelligence about an imminent al Qaeda attack. And we had a very good reason to believe he knew about it. And if we knew what he knew, we could stop it. If we thought we could glean a critical piece of information by use of sodium pentathol, would we be permitted to do so?

Less hypothetically, there is waterboarding, a terrifying and deeply shocking torture technique in which the prisoner has his face exposed to water in a way that gives the feeling of drowning. According to CIA sources cited by ABC News, Khalid Sheikh Mohammed "was able to last between two and 2 1/2 minutes before begging to confess." Should we regret having done that? Should we abolish by law that practice, so that it could never be used on the next Khalid Sheikh Mohammed having thus gotten his confession?

And what if he possessed information with less imminent implications? Say we had information about a cell that he had helped found or direct, and that cell was planning some major attack and we needed information about the identity and location of its members. A rational moral calculus might not permit measures as extreme as the nuke-in-Manhattan scenario, but would surely permit measures beyond mere psychological pressure.

Such a determination would not be made with an untroubled conscience. It would be troubled because there is no denying the monstrous evil that is any form of torture. And there is no denying how corrupting it can be to the individuals and society that practice it. But elected leaders, responsible above all for the protection of their citizens, have the obligation to tolerate their own sleepless nights by doing what is necessary—and only what is necessary, nothing more—to get information that could prevent mass murder.

We Need Rules

Given the gravity of the decision, if we indeed cross the Rubicon [a metaphor for a point of no return]—as we must—we need rules. The problem with the McCain amendment is that once you have gone public with a blanket ban on all forms of coercion, it is going to be very difficult to publicly carve out exceptions. The [George W.] Bush administration is to be faulted for having attempted such a codification with the kind of secrecy, lack of coherence, and lack of strict enforcement that led us to the McCain reaction.

What to do at this late date? Begin, as McCain does, by banning all forms of coercion or inhuman treatment by anyone serving in the military—an absolute ban on torture by all military personnel everywhere. We do not want a private somewhere making these fine distinctions about ticking and slow-fuse time bombs. We don't even want colonels or generals making them. It would be best for the morale, discipline, and honor of the Armed Forces for the United States to maintain an absolute prohibition, both to simplify their task in making decisions and to offer them whatever reciprocal treatment they might receive from those who capture them—although I have no illusion that any anti-torture provision will soften the heart of a single jihadist holding a knife to the throat of a captured American soldier. We would impose this restriction on ourselves for our own reasons of military discipline and military honor.

Ban Torture with Two Exceptions

Outside the military, however, I would propose, contra McCain, a ban against all forms of torture, coercive interrogation, and inhuman treatment, except in two contingencies: (1) the ticking time bomb and (2) the slower-fuse high-level terrorist (such as KSM [Khalid Sheikh Mohammed]). Each contingency would have its own set of rules. In the case of the ticking time bomb, the rules would be relatively simple: Nothing rationally related to getting accurate information would be ruled out. The case of the high-value suspect with slow-fuse information is more complicated. The principle would be that the level of inhumanity of the measures used (moral honesty is essential here—we would be using measures that are by definition inhumane) would be proportional to the need and value of the information. Interrogators would be constrained to use the least inhumane treatment necessary relative to the magnitude and imminence of the evil being prevented and the importance of the knowledge being obtained.

These exceptions to the no-torture rule would not be granted to just any nonmilitary interrogators, or anyone with CIA credentials. They would be reserved for highly specialized agents who are experts and experienced in interrogation, and who are known not to abuse it for the satisfaction of a kind of sick sadomasochism Lynndie England [U.S. soldier convicted of abusing prisoners] and her cohorts indulged in at Abu Ghraib. Nor would they be acting on their own. They would be required to obtain written permission for such interrogations from the highest political authorities in the country (cabinet level) or from a quasi-judicial body modeled on the Foreign Intelligence Surveillance Court (which permits what would ordinarily be illegal searches and seizures in the war on terror). Or, if the bomb was truly ticking and there was no time, the interrogators would be allowed to act on their own, but would require post facto authorization within, say, 24 hours of their interrogation, so that they knew that whatever they did would be subject to review by others and be justified only under the most stringent terms.

One of the purposes of these justifications would be to establish that whatever extreme measures are used are for reasons of nothing but information. Historically, the torture of prisoners has been done for a variety of reasons apart from information, most prominently reasons of justice or revenge. We do not do that. We should not do that. Ever. Khalid Sheikh Mohammed, murderer of 2,973 innocents, is surely deserving of the most extreme suffering day and night for the rest of his life. But it is neither our role nor our right to be the agents of that suffering. Vengeance is mine, sayeth the Lord. His, not ours. Torture is a terrible and monstrous thing, as degrading and morally corrupting to those who practice it as any conceivable human activity including its moral twin, capital punishment.

If Khalid Sheikh Mohammed knew nothing, or if we had reached the point where his knowledge had been exhausted, I'd be perfectly prepared to throw him into a nice, comfortable Manhattan cell and give him a trial to determine what would be fit and just punishment. But as long as he had useful information, things would be different.

Sometimes Torture Works

Very different. And it simply will not do to take refuge in the claim that all of the above discussion is superfluous because torture never works anyway. Would that this were true. Unfortunately, on its face, this is nonsense. Is one to believe that in the entire history of human warfare, no combatant has ever received useful information by the use of pressure, torture, or any other kind of inhuman treatment? It may indeed be true that torture is not a reliable tool. But that is very different from saying that it is *never* useful.

The monstrous thing about torture is that sometimes it does work. In 1994, 19-year-old Israeli corporal Nachshon Waxman was kidnapped by Palestinian terrorists. The Israelis captured the driver of the car used in the kidnapping and tortured him in order to find where Waxman was being held. Yitzhak Rabin, prime minister and peacemaker, admitted that they tortured him in a way that went even beyond the '87 guidelines for "coercive interrogation" later struck down by the Israeli Supreme Court as too harsh. The driver talked. His information was accurate. The Israelis found Waxman. "If we'd been so careful to follow the ['87] Landau Commission [which *allowed* coercive interrogation]," explained Rabin, "we would never have found out where Waxman was being held."

In the Waxman case, I would have done precisely what Rabin did. (The fact that Waxman's Palestinian captors killed him during the Israeli rescue raid makes the case doubly tragic, but changes nothing of the moral calculus.) Faced with a similar choice, an American president would have a similar obligation. To do otherwise—to give up the chance to find your soldier lest you sully yourself by authorizing torture of the person who possesses potentially lifesaving information—is a deeply immoral betrayal of a soldier and countryman. Not as cosmically immoral as permitting a city of one's countrymen to perish, as in the Ethics 101 case. But it remains, nonetheless, a case of moral abdication—of a kind rather parallel to that of the principled pacifist. There is much to admire in those who refuse on principle ever to take up arms under any conditions. But that does not make pure pacifism, like no-torture absolutism, any less a form of moral foolishness, tinged with moral vanity. Not reprehensible, only deeply reproachable and supremely impracticable. People who hold such beliefs are deserving of a certain respect. But they are not to be put in positions of authority. One should be grateful for the saintly among us. And one should be vigilant that they not get to make the decisions upon which the lives of others depend.

> "The United States should strive to be a leader and set an example for the rest of the world in its commitment to women and expanding women's rights."

The United States Should Ratify the Treaty to Protect Women's Human Rights

Working Group on Ratification of the United Nations Convention on the Elimination of All Forms of Discrimination Against Women (CEDAW)

In the following viewpoint, the Working Group on Ratification of the U.N. Convention on the Elimination of All Forms of Discrimination Against Women (CEDAW), proclaims that the United States should ratify the treaty to protect women's rights. The authors point out the accomplishments of the treaty in improving women's lives worldwide, but they also say that much remains to be done. The United States could help improve women's lives by ratifying CEDAW, say the authors. As of late 2007, the United States had still not ratified CEDAW. The Working Group on Ratification of CEDAW is a group of 195 national

"The Treaty for the Rights of Women would amplify the U.S. voice in saving women's lives worldwide: Why a Treaty? Why Now?" *UN Convention on the Elimination of All Forms of Discrimination Against Women (CEDAW)*, www.womenstreaty.org. Reproduced by permission.

nongovernmental organizations engaged in outreach and education to achieve U.S. ratification of the Treaty for the Rights of Women.

As you read, consider the following questions:

1. When was CEDAW created?
2. Which countries saw increases in literacy rates because of CEDAW?
3. Does ratification of CEDAW require a change in law?

A mericans are united in supporting basic human rights for women around the world. A global consensus is growing on the need to address the most pressing issues affecting women and girls, especially on providing access to education and health care and ending violence.

Treaty for Rights of Women

—The Treaty for the Rights of Women, formally named the Convention on the Elimination of All Forms of Discrimination Against Women (CEDAW), is the most comprehensive international agreement on basic rights of women. The treaty has been ratified by over 184 nations and has become an important tool for partnerships among nations to end human rights abuses and promote the health and well-being of girls.

—In many countries worldwide that have ratified the treaty, women have worked with their governments in partnership to change inequitable laws: to help girls receive a primary education; to enable women to get micro-loans to set up small businesses; to stop sex slavery; to improve health care services; to secure the right to own or inherit property; and to protect women and girls against violence. . . .

Overwhelming Support

Over 190 U.S. religious, civic and community organizations support the ratification of CEDAW, such as the [labor union] AFL-CIO, the United Methodist Church, and the League of Women Voters. Research shows that the American public, when informed of CEDAW, also supports U.S. ratification. Ratification of CEDAW could help to advance political and economic equality for women in the U.S., as women in this country have not yet achieved full equality. U.S. women comprise only 14 percent of the Congress and 22 percent of state legislatures, are paid $.70 for every $1 a man makes for the same work and face repeated attacks on their reproductive rights.

Although the United States government has not yet ratified CEDAW, action has been taken in cities, counties and states across the U.S. For example, the city of San Francisco, California, enacted a local ordinance in 1998 based on the convention's principles. The ordinance requires the city to protect women's human rights, including the elimination of discrimination against women and girls.

Women Engaging Globally,
www.centerwomenpolicy.org,
www.lwv.org, www.wedo.org.

—The Treaty has always enjoyed bipartisan support in the United States, but has never come before the full Senate for a vote. This unfinished business puts the United States in the company of only a handful of nations that have not ratified the treaty, including Iran, Sudan, and Somalia. As a party to the treaty, the Untied States will have a seat at the table where decisions are made about women's lives around the world and, with all other ratifying nations, will file regular reports on our progress.

—U.S. law already complies with the treaty, and to ratify it will not require the passage of a single new law. *The Treaty for the Rights of Women provides us with a useful framework for improving the human rights and the rule of law internationally.*

The United States should strive to be a leader and set an example for the rest of the world in its commitment to women and expanding women's rights. The Senate and President George W. Bush should lead the United States toward joining the overwhelming majority of other countries in ratifying the Treaty for the Rights of Women, adding our strength to the work of ensuring basic human rights for women everywhere.

An Important Tool to End Abuse of Women

The Convention to End All Forms of Discrimination Against Women (CEDAW) is the most comprehensive international agreement on the basic human rights of women. Created in 1979, it is an important tool for all those who seek to end abuses of women and girls throughout the globe.

Because of the CEDAW Treaty, millions of girls are now receiving primary education who were previously denied access; measures have been taken against sex slavery, domestic violence and trafficking of women; women's health care services have improved, saving lives during pregnancy and childbirth; and millions of women have secured loans or the right to own or inherit property.

Nations that ratify the treaty commit to overcoming barriers to discrimination against women in the areas of legal rights, education, employment, health care, politics and finance. Like all human rights treaties, the CEDAW Treaty sets benchmarks within traditional enforcement mechanisms that respect sovereignty and democracy. In many of the 182 countries that have ratified the treaty, it has guided the passage and enforcement of national laws. For example:

- Uganda, South Africa, Brazil, Australia and others have incorporated treaty provisions into their constitutions and domestic legal codes;

- Ukraine, Nepal, Thailand and the Philippines all passed laws to curb sexual trafficking;

- India developed national guidelines on workplace sexual assault after the Supreme Court, in ruling on a major rape case, found that CEDAW required such protections;

- Nicaragua, Jordan, Egypt and Guinea all saw significant increases in literacy rates after improving access to education for girls and women;

- Australia and Luxembourg created health campaigns promoting awareness and prevention of breast and cervical cancers; and

- After ratification, Colombia made domestic violence a crime and required legal protection for its victims.

Much remains to be done:

- Sex trafficking: 80% of the estimated 600,000 to 800,000 victims trafficked across international borders are female and nearly half are under the age of 18;

- Education: two-thirds of the world's 771 million illiterate adults are women;

- Maternal mortality: 500,000 women die each year from pregnancy-related complications;

- HIV/AIDS: women are four times more vulnerable than men, and 1.3 million die each year;

- Violence: an estimated 25 to 39 percent of all women experience domestic violence;

- Discrimination: millions of women lack full legal and political rights;

- Poverty: 70% of the world's 1.3 billion people living in dire poverty are women; and

- Female genital mutilation: 130 million women are victims.

How Would U.S. Ratification Help Women Around the World?

The United States has long been a world leader on human rights. But, U.S. failure to ratify the treaty allows other countries to divert attention away from their neglect of women and undermines the powerful principle that human rights of women are universal across all cultures, nations, and religions. Until the United States ratifies CEDAW, our country cannot credibly demand that others live up to their obligations under this treaty. Our failure to ratify puts us in the company of Sudan, Iran and Somalia; every other industrialized country has ratified the treaty.

Ratification does not require any change in U.S. law and would be a powerful statement of our continuing commitment to ending discrimination against women worldwide. It would allow us to join with other countries to work toward the common goal of women's equality. The U.S. already has laws consistent with the CEDAW Treaty. Under the terms of the treaty, the U.S. would submit regular reports to an advisory committee, which would provide an important opportunity to spotlight our best practices and assess where we can do better.

The United States has a bipartisan tradition of support for international standards through human rights treaties. Presidents [Ronald] Reagan, [George H.W.] Bush and [Bill] Clinton ratified similar treaties on genocide, torture, race and civil and political rights. This treaty continues that proud tradition.

"At its best, CEDAW is unnecessary. At its worst, CEDAW unravels America's families and forces women to model themselves after global feminists' ideal image."

The United States Should Not Ratify the Treaty to Protect Women's Human Rights

Janice Shaw Crouse

In this viewpoint, Janice Shaw Crouse contends that there are serious flaws in the U.N. Convention on the Elimination of All Forms of Discrimination Against Women (CEDAW) and that the U.S. should not ratify the treaty. Doing so, claims Crouse, would undermine American family values and could lead to increases in abortion and prostitution. Furthermore, ratifying the treaty is unconstitutional says Crouse. Janice Shaw Crouse is an author and former speech writer for President George W. Bush. Concerned Women of America is a women's organization that brings biblical principles into public policy.

Janice Shaw Crouse, "Not Only Is the Convention on the Elimination of All Forms of Discrimination Against Women (CEDAW) Treaty Not Necessary, Its Ratification Would Challenge and Undermine the Laws and Culture of the United States," *Concerned Women For America*, January 15, 2007. Reproduced by permission.

As you read, consider the following questions:

1. What do Articles 5 and 16 of CEDAW affirm?
2. What did the CEDAW Committee say on January 25, 2001?
3. What must countries do after signing CEDAW?

Not only is the *Convention on the Elimination of All Forms of Discrimination Against Women* (CEDAW) treaty not necessary, its ratification would challenge and undermine the laws and culture of the United States.

Unlike hundreds of other nations that sign and ignore international agreements, the United States takes treaty agreements seriously. According to Article VI, Section 2, of the U.S. Constitution, treaties—along with the Constitution and United States laws—are "the supreme Law of the Land." Our founding fathers believed that any ratified treaty should be constitutional.

Further, the U.N. Committee on the Elimination of Discrimination against Women requires countries that ratify CEDAW to report to the committee every four years on how their country is implementing the treaty.

Egregious Provisions of CEDAW:

1. *CEDAW undermines the traditional family structure* in the United States and in other nations that respect the family. The preamble states, "A change in the traditional role of men as well as the role of women in society and in the family is needed to achieve full equality between men and women." Article 5a would require the United States government to "take all appropriate action" to:

"Modify the social and cultural patterns of conduct of men and women, with a view to achieving the elimination of prejudices ... based on ... stereotyped roles for men and women." The treaty also calls individual American states to give up authority in family law, allowing the federal government to take over family law.

2. *CEDAW is a global Equal Rights Amendment,* a tool for radical feminists, who work to deny any distinctions between men and women.

CEDAW defines discrimination as "any distinction . . . on the basis of sex," in "any . . . field." In other words, no one is allowed to recognize the wonderful differences between men and women. Even in the most personal of relationships—family, marriage and religious. It requires governments to "modify the social and cultural patterns of conduct of men and women with a view to achieving the elimination of . . . all . . . practices which are based on . . . stereotyped roles for men and women."

According to this document, *any* "distinction, exclusion or restriction" could be changed if a woman claims that such distinctions "nullify her recognition, enjoyment or exercise . . . of human rights and fundamental freedoms." This language is far too vague and would invite an avalanche of frivolous lawsuits in the United States.

3. *CEDAW undercuts the proper role of parents in child rearing.* Articles 5 and 16 affirm that in family matters "the interests of the children shall be paramount." Who decides what is in a child's "best interest"? What penalty would result from violating the "best interest" of the child? This superficial, feel-good statement subordinates every family member, regardless of the issue or circumstance.

4. *CEDAW would guarantee global abortion policy.* Articles 12 and 14 section 2b seek "to ensure, on a basis of equality of men and women, access to health care services, including those related to family planning," rhetoric which means open access to abortion services.

5. *CEDAW would captivate our children to the Left's agenda* through a U.N. mandate. Single-sex schools could be discouraged and eliminated because their "perspective" on gender is

not acceptable to the international government. Taxpayers could be forced to pay the high cost of "gender neutralizing" all textbooks and school programs. America could become a nation of androgynous children who are not *allowed* to believe that any gender differences exist beyond the external.

For example, the U.N. Committee on CEDAW recommended that the Romanian government "place priority on the review and revision of teaching materials, textbooks and school curricula, especially for primary- and secondary-level education." It called upon Austria's government to "integrate gender studies and feminist research in university curricula and research programs."

6. *CEDAW encourages global prostitution to the detriment of needy women.* Article 6 states that countries that have ratified CEDAW "shall take all appropriate measures, including legislation, to suppress all forms of traffic in women and exploitation of prostitution in women." Tragically, the CEDAW Committee has deviated completely from the original intention of the document regarding prostitution.

Article 11, section 1(c) of the treaty upholds "the right to free choice of profession and employment." The Committee has included "voluntary" prostitution in that "free choice"—to the detriment of needy women around the world.

7. *Twenty-three international "experts" would govern U.S. women's rights through the Committee to Eliminate Discrimination Against Women.* CEDAW Part V (Articles 17-22) outlines the creation of a Committee to oversee the implementation of CEDAW in every signatory nation. This Committee consists of "23 experts of high and moral standing and competence in the field covered by the Convention" whom representatives of the Convention signatories elect. This, in essence, places the welfare and well being of American women and families at the mercy of 23 individuals, among whom the United States might not even have a voice.

This committee currently includes representatives from China (which forcibly aborts women) and Cuba (which murders women who attempt to escape the island). Ironically, eight countries that the State Department recently identified as in Tier 2 Watch for sexual trafficking have representatives sitting on the U.N. CEDAW Committee.

Other countries that ratified CEDAW and have been on the committee in the past and could be again are Iraq, North Korea and Saudi Arabia.

Cause for Concern

- February 3, 1999, the CEDAW Committee said that it was "concerned that prostitution . . . is illegal in China" and it "recommends the decriminalization of prostitution in China."

- January 31, 2000, the CEDAW Committee criticized Belarus for "the continuing reintroduction of such symbols as a Mothers' Day. . . ."

- August 12, 1997, the CEDAW Committee criticized Slovenia because "less than 30 per cent of children under three years of age . . . were in formal day care."

- January 25, 2001, the CEDAW Committee "expressed concern that women's motherhood role was taking precedence over their professional and individual development" in Uzbekistan.

- January 21, 2000, complained to Luxembourg about its "stereotypical attitudes that tend to portray men as heads of households and breadwinners, and women primarily as mothers and homemakers."

- July 1, 1999 the CEDAW Committee criticized Ireland for its constitution for "promoting a stereotypical view of the role of women in the home and as mothers."

CEDAW Is a Totalitarian Piece of Social Engineering

Now that the party of death has retaken control of congress, battles over funding of embryonic stem cell research, chemical abortifacients, contraception, sex education, special privileges for homosexuals, and other such controversies will ensue over the next two years. The fight over an obscure international treaty could be just as important, if not more so, than these others even though few people have ever heard of CEDAW.

The pompously named CEDAW, the Convention on the Elimination of All Forms of Discrimination Against Women, sounds on its face not to be too bad, just clumsy and utopian. Yet it is a totalitarian piece of social engineering that aims to do everything from legalize abortion-on-demand worldwide to abolish Mother's Day (no joke).

Steven Mosher, "CEDAW Makes a Comeback,"
Life Issues.net, www.lifeissues.net.

- July 1, 1999 the CEDAW Committee criticized Ireland for "the influence of the Church . . . in attitudes and stereotypes but also in official state policy."

- April 12, 1994 the CEDAW Committee told Libya "the interpretation of the Koran had to be reviewed in the light of the provisions of the Convention. . . ."

Points to Consider

No real majority in the Senate is needed to ratify CEDAW. The U.S. Constitution allows the president to enter into treaties with two-thirds Senate approval. It also requires the Senate to have a quorum, a majority (51), present to conduct business. Thus, with 51 senators present, CEDAW would need a minimum of 34 approving senators to ratify it. You can guess who—depending on whether they survive the next election—would attend the vote were CEDAW to come to the Senate floor.

CEDAW legally binds every signatory country to implement its provisions. After signing, each country must submit an initial report with a detailed and comprehensive description of the state of its women, "a benchmark against which subsequent progress can be measured." This initial report should include legislative, judicial, administrative and other measures the signatory nation has adopted to comply with CEDAW. The country must submit follow-up reports at least every four years.

Radical feminists in Western nations are using poor women's disadvantages to push an agenda of sexual and reproductive rights for females as young as age 10. Poor women in developing nations are fighting for the basic needs of everyday life—education and literacy, access to health care for basic medical needs, i.e. nutrition, etc. Hiding under the guise of "human rights," and veiling their intentions with appeals for needy women in developing nations, feminists insist CEDAW is necessary.

The *Convention on the Elimination of All Forms of Discrimination Against Women* is flawed. The U.S. Senate must not ratify it. At its best, CEDAW is unnecessary. At its worst, CEDAW unravels America's families and forces women to model themselves after global feminists' ideal image.

Periodical Bibliography

The following articles have been selected to supplement the diverse views presented in this chapter.

Tom Carney

"Americans, Especially Catholics, Approve of Torture," *National Catholic Reporter*, March 24, 2006.

Frank Chalk

"'Atrocity Crimes' and the Darfur Crisis," *Montreal Institute for Genocide and Human Rights Studies*, October 26, 2005. www.migs.concordia.ca

The Economist

"Let the Child Live; International Criminal Court (America's Changing Attitude Towards the International Criminal Court)," January 27, 2007.

Shadi Mokhtari

"Human Rights in the Post-September 11th Era: Between Hegemony and Emancipation," *Muslim World Journal of Human Rights*, 2006.

Barack Obama and Sam Brownback

"U.S. Policy Adrift on Darfur," *Washington Post*, December 27, 2005.

Priti Patel

"Abuse Cases in a Legal Twilight," *The News and Observer Online*, February 15, 2007.

Deborah Pearlstein

"Who's Afraid of International Law?" *The American Prospect Online*, April 5, 2005

Gabor Rona

"Constitutional and Policy Implications of Military Tribunals for Terrorism Detainees Remarks at the Boston Federalist Society," *Human Rights First*. February 2, 2006, www.humanrightsfirst.org.

John Washburn

"United States' Slow March to Justice," *The Monitor*, May 2007.

For Further Discussion

Chapter 1

1. What do you think the UN's Integrated Regional Information Networks (IRIN) thinks about Jieh-Yung Lo's assertion that Asian values are different than the values expressed in the Universal Declaration of Human Rights?

2. What do you think Jieh-Yung Lo thinks about the UN IRIN's assertion that the culturally relative concept of human rights denies rights to some groups of people? Do you think that if community rights are placed above individual rights, as Lo contends Asian cultures do, that some groups of people are denied rights? Explain.

Chapter 2

1. The Asian Pacific Research Network (APRN) contends that globalization violates many human rights, while Daniel Griswold argues that globalization leads to respect for human rights. After reading their viewpoints, do you think globalization helps or hurts human rights? Support your answer with information from the viewpoints.

2. Why do you think Azam Kamguian calls for the establishment of secular states? What do you think Louay Safi thinks about secular rule of law?

3. Analyze the viewpoints of the U.S. State Department and the Information Office of the State Council of the People's Republic of China. Compare and contrast the sources of information and the basis that each author uses to support their argument. Are the examples of human rights violations that China uses really human rights violations? Explain.

Chapter 3

1. Silvano M. Tomasi says that the United Nations is a necessary organization, while Joseph Loconte contends that the UN is corrupt and ineffective. Do you think Loconte believes the UN is unnecessary or just that the UN needs reforming? After reading the viewpoints, do you think the UN is a necessary organization to prevent human rights abuses? Why or why not?

2. Anne Bayefsky contends that the United Nations' treaties are an effective way of bringing nation-states into compliance with human rights norms. But, Jack Goldsmith and Eric Posner believe that the state of human rights is not impacted by the establishment of treaties. Whose argument do you think is stronger? Do you think it's possible to believe someone makes a compelling argument but to not agree with their assertion? Whose argument is more general and whose is more specific? Explain.

Chapter 4

1. Briony MacPhee says the International Criminal Court (ICC) is consistent with "conservative" American ideals. What does this mean and why do you think she argues this? Do you think Brett Schaefer and the Heritage Foundation reflect conservative American ideals? Do you think MacPhee's viewpoint adequately addresses Brett Schaefer's concerns about the ICC?

2. After reading the viewpoints of Justin Raimondo and the editors of *The New Republic*, do you think there is anything they agree upon? If so, what?

3. Between Jimmy Carter and Charles Krauthammer, which argument is more convincing and why? What do Carter and Krauthammer each think about the reliability of information gained through torture?

4. The Working Group on Ratification of the UN Convention on the Elimination of All Forms of Discrimination Against

Women (CEDAW) proclaims that the United States should ratify the treaty to protect women's rights. However, Janet Crouse believes CEDAW is detrimental to women. After reading the viewpoints, why do you think the United States should or should not ratify CEDAW? Support your assertion.

5. Which of the viewpoints in Chapter 4 contend that the United States should not follow the lead of world opinion and do what a majority of other countries are doing, i.e., by signing a treaty, joining a group, instituting a policy, etc.? Which viewpoints use the argument that the United States should sign a treaty, join a group, or institute a policy, because what the United States does impacts human rights around the world?

Organizations to Contact

The editors have compiled the following list of organizations concerned with the issues debated in this book. The descriptions are derived from materials provided by the organizations. All have publications or information available for interested readers. The list was compiled on the date of publication of the present volume; the information provided here may change. Be aware that many organizations take several weeks or longer to respond to inquiries, so allow as much time as possible.

Amnesty International (AI)
5 Penn Plaza, 14th floor, New York, NY 10001
(212) 807-8400 • fax: (212) 463-9193
e-mail: admin-us@aiusa.org
Web site: www.amnestyusa.org

Amnesty International (AI) is a worldwide movement of people who campaign for internationally recognized human rights. AI investigates and campaigns against human rights violations around the world. The organization undertakes research and actions focused on preventing and ending grave abuses of the rights to physical and mental integrity, freedom of conscience and expression, and freedom from discrimination. AI publishes a monthly magazine called *The Wire* as well as numerous reports and documents about human rights around the world.

Carnegie Council for Ethics in International Affairs
Merrill House, 170 East 64th St., New York, NY 10021-7478
(212) 838-4120 • fax: (212) 752-2432
e-mail: info@cceia.org
Web site: www.cceia.org

The Carnegie Council is an international organization promoting ethical leadership on issues of war, peace, and global social justice. The Carnegie Council's mission is to be the voice for ethics in international policy. The council convenes agenda-setting forums and creates educational opportunities and information resources for a worldwide audience of teachers and students, journalists, international affairs professionals, and concerned citizens.

The council offers a broad array of reference material including a quarterly journal, *Ethics & International Affairs* and the *Insider*, an electronic newsletter.

The Carter Center

One Copenhill, 453 Freedom Pkwy., Atlanta, GA   30307
(800) 550-3560
e-mail: carterweb@emory.edu
Web site: www.cartercenter.org

The Carter Center was founded in 1982 by U.S. President Jimmy Carter and former First Lady Rosalynn Carter. The Carter Center, in partnership with Emory University, is guided by a fundamental commitment to human rights and the alleviation of human suffering; it seeks to prevent and resolve conflicts, enhance freedom and democracy, and improve health for people around the globe. The Carter Center News and Information Center provides both breaking Carter Center news and background information on human rights, disease control and prevention, democracy, and on international affairs.

Center for Economic and Social Rights (CESR)

162 Montague St., 3rd Floor, Brooklyn, NY   11201
(718) 237-9145 • fax: (718) 237-9147
e-mail: rights@cesr.org
Web site: www.cesr.org

The Center for Economic and Social Rights (CESR) was established in 1993 to promote social justice through human rights. The CESR promotes economic and social rights as contained in the Universal Declaration of Human Rights. The organization protects the rights of all human beings to housing, education, health and a healthy environment, food, work, and an adequate standard of living. CESR publishes various articles, fact sheets, reports, and training materials.

Coalition for the International Criminal Court (CICC)

c/o WFM, 708 3rd Ave., 24th Floor, New York, NY 10017
(212) 687-2863 • fax: (212) 599-1332
e-mail: cicc@iccnow.org
Web site: www.iccnow.org

The Coalition for the International Criminal Court (CICC) is an international network of thousands of civil society organizations and hundreds of nongovernmental organizations (NGOs) dedicated to the establishment, acceptance, and implementation of the International Criminal Court. The CICC's objectives include: promoting awareness of the ICC and Rome Statute; facilitating the effective participation of civil society in the sessions of the Assembly of States Parties; promoting universal acceptance and ratification of and accession to the Rome Statute and the full implementation of the treaty's obligations into national law; monitoring and supporting the full establishment of the Court; and promoting international support for the ICC. The CICC publishes numerous documents including the magazine, *The Monitor*, and various newsletters and fact sheets.

Freedom House

1301 Connecticut Ave. NW, Floor 6, Washington, DC 20036
(202) 296-5101 • fax: (202) 293-2840
e-mail: info@freedomhouse.org
Web site: www.freedomhouse.org

Freedom House is an independent nongovernmental organization that supports the expansion of freedom in the world. The organization believes that freedom is possible only in democratic political systems in which the governments are accountable to their own people; the rule of law prevails; and freedoms of expression, association, belief, and respect for the rights of minorities and women are guaranteed. Freedom

House supports nonviolent civic initiatives in societies where freedom is denied or under threat and stands in opposition to ideas and forces that challenge the right of all people to be free. Freedom House publishes several annual reports including, *Freedom in the World, Freedom of the Press, Nations in Transit,* and *Countries at the Crossroads.*

Genocide Watch
PO Box 809, Washington, DC   20044
(703) 448-0222
e-mail: info@genocidewatch.org
Web site: www.genocidewatch.org

Genocide Watch exists to predict, prevent, stop, and punish genocide and other forms of mass murder. The organization seeks to raise awareness about genocide and influence public policy concerning potential and actual genocide. The organization's Web site links many antigenocide resources and articles and information about genocides or potential genocides around the world. The organization also issues *Genocide Alerts*, which depending on the situation, may be classified as a genocide watch, genocide warning, or genocide emergency.

Human Rights Watch (HRW)
350 Fifth Ave., 34th Floor, New York, NY   10118-3299
(212) 290-4700 • fax: (212) 736-1300
e-mail: hrwnyc@hrw.org
Web site: www.hrw.org

Human Rights Watch (HRW) is the largest United States-based human rights organization. It seeks to prevent discrimination, to uphold political freedom, to protect people from inhumane conduct in wartime, and to bring offenders to justice. HRW investigates, exposes, and reports on human rights abuses around the world. One of the goals of the organization is to bring human rights abuses to the public's attention for the purpose of embarrassing abusive governments. HRW publishes myriad reports on human rights themes, such as children's rights, women's rights, and HIV/AIDS. Additionally, HRW issues reports on the state of human rights in each region of the world.

International Crisis Group (ICG)
420 Lexington Avenue, Suite 2640, New York, NY   10170
(212) 813-0820 • fax: (212) 813-0825
Web site: www.crisisgroup.org

The International Crisis Group (ICG) is an independent, nonprofit, nongovernmental organization working through field-based analysis and advocacy to prevent and resolve deadly conflict. ICG's political analysts are located within or close by countries at risk of outbreak, escalation, or recurrence of violent conflict. Based on information and assessments from the field, ICG produces analytical reports containing practical recommendations targeted at key international decision makers. ICG also publishes *CrisisWatch*, a twelve-page monthly bulletin, providing regular updates on the state of the most significant situations of conflict or potential conflict around the world.

Reset Dialogues on Civilizations
Via di San Pantaleo, 66, Rome   00186
    Italy
+39 06 68407012 • Fax: +39 06 68807262
e-mail: doc@resetdoc.org
Web site: www.resetdoc.org

The goals of Reset Dialogues on Civilizations, the international cultural association, are the promotion of dialogue and the culture of dialogue in the world; the promotion of the culture of freedom, of human rights, and of the rule of law; the reduction of the tensions that might arise from cultural differences; and the encouragement of the conditions for pacific resolutions of conflicts. In order to achieve its aims, the organization contributes through debates, meetings, seminars, and publications; to promote cultural understanding on the basis of reciprocity and equal dignity; to oppose exclusivist and intolerant trends of ethnic nationalism, racism, religious fanaticism, and radicalism—which often lead to violence, terrorism, and conflicts. Reset Dialogues on Civilizations promotes publications that suit the association's goals and circulates news on social activities and pertaining topics, both through the Web site and through a monthly newsletter in English and Italian.

Save the Children
54 Wilton Rd., Westport, CT   06880
(800) 728-3843
e-mail: twebster@savechildren.org
Web site: www.savethechildren.org

Save the Children is the leading independent organization creating real and lasting change for children in need in the United States and around the world. It is a member of the International Save the Children Alliance, comprising twenty-eight national Save the Children organizations working in more than 110 countries to ensure the well-being of children. The organization publishes a newsletter and various research reports including an annual *State of the World's Mothers*.

United Nations (UN)
First Avenue at 46th St., New York, NY   10017
e-mail: inquiries2@un.org
Web sites of interest: www.un.org/Pubs/CyberSchoolBus/
humanrights/qna.htm

The United Nations system is a vast organization comprised of more than thirty affiliated organizations and bodies that seek to solve the myriad of problems challenging humanity. The UN and its family of organizations work to promote respect for human rights, protect the environment, fight disease, and reduce poverty. UN agencies define the standards for safe and efficient air travel and help improve telecommunications and enhance consumer protection. The United Nations leads the international campaigns against drug trafficking and terrorism. Throughout the world, the UN and its agencies assist refugees, set up programs to clear land mines, help expand food production, and lead the fight against AIDS. In regard to human rights issues, the UN publishes many books and several periodicals such as the *UN Chronicle*, a quarterly publication that provides in-depth coverage and information on the UN General Assembly, and *Africa Renewal*, which provides up-to-date information and analysis of the major economic and development challenges facing Africa today.

United Nations Children's Fund (UNICEF)
UNICEF House, 3 United Nations Plaza
New York, NY 10017
(212) 326-7000 • fax: (212) 887-7465
e-mail: information@unicefusa.org
Web site: www.unicef.org

The United Nations Children's Fund (UNICEF) was created (as the United Nation's International Children's Emergency Fund) on December 11, 1946. UNICEF provides long-term humanitarian and developmental assistance to children and mothers in developing countries. Guided by the Convention on the Rights of the Child, the organization works for children's rights, their survival, development, and protection. Each year UNICEF publishes *The State of the World's Children* and *Progress for Children*, as well as several other reports on children's human rights, such as *Africa's Orphaned and Vulnerable Children: Children Afflicted by Aids* and *Pneumonia: The Forgotten Killer of Children*. UNICEF also publishes an electronic newsletter at least once each month.

The United States Institute of Peace (USIP)
1200 17th St. NW, Washington, DC 20036
(202) 457-1700 • fax: (202) 429-6063
Web site: www.usip.org

The United States Institute of Peace (USIP) is an independent, nonpartisan, national institution established and funded by the U.S. Congress. Its goals are to help prevent and resolve violent conflicts, promote post-conflict stability and development, and increase peace-building capacity, tools, and intellectual capital worldwide. The institute does this by empowering others with knowledge, skills, and resources, as well as by directly engaging in peacebuilding efforts around the world. The USIP regularly publishes an array of comprehensive analysis and policy recommendations on current international affairs issues, especially on the prevention and resolution of conflict.

Youth for Human Rights International (YHRI)
1954 Hillhurst Ave. # 416, Los Angeles, CA   90027
(323) 661-5799
e-mail: info@youthforhumanrights.org
Web site: www.youthforhumanrights.org

Youth for Human Rights International (YHRI) is an independent non-profit corporation headquartered in Los Angeles, with the purpose to educate people in the Universal Declaration of Human Rights so they become valuable advocates for tolerance and peace. YHRI works with human rights advocates, legislators, teachers, police, and humanitarians to encourage young people to learn and champion human rights. YHRI holds events and produces instructional tools to raise human rights awareness such as music videos, public service announcements, and the *UNITED Human Rights Handbook*.

Bibliography of Books

Peter Balakian   *The Burning Tigris: The Armenian Genocide and America's Response.* New York: HarperCollins, 2003.

Peter Berkowitz   *Terrorism, the Laws of War, and the Constitution: Debating the Enemy Combatant Cases.* Stanford, CA: Hoover Institution Press, 2005.

Robert D. Bullard   *The Quest for Environmental Justice: Human Rights and the Politics of Pollution.* San Francisco: Sierra Club, 2005.

Anthony Chase and Amr Hamzawy   *Human Rights in the Arab World: Independent Voices.* Philadelphia: University of Pennsylvania Press, 2007.

Don Cheadle and John Prendergast   *Not on Our Watch: The Mission to End Genocide in Darfur and Beyond.* New York: Hyperion, 2007.

David Cole   *Enemy Aliens: Double Standards and Constitutional Freedoms in the War on Terrorism.* New York: New Press, 2003.

Alex Conte, Scott Davidson, and Richard Burchill   *Defining Civil and Political Rights: The Jurisprudence of the United Nations Human Rights Committee.* Burlington, VT: Ashgate, 2004.

Alan M. Dershowitz   *Rights From Wrongs: Secular Theory of the Origins of Rights.* New York: Basic Books, 2004.

Linda Diebel   *Betrayed: The Assassination of Digna Ochoa*. New York: Carroll & Graf, 2005.

Robert Gellately *The Specter of Genocide: Mass Murder and Ben Kiernan in Historical Perspective*. New York: Cambridge University Press, 2003.

Martin   *What's Wrong With Children's Rights.* Guggenheim   Cambridge, MA: Harvard University Press. 2005.

Linda M. Fasulo *An Insider's Guide to the UN*. New Haven, CT: Yale University Press, 2004.

Michael Ignatieff *The Lesser Evil: Political Ethics in an Age of Terror*. Princeton, NJ: Princeton University Press, 2004.

Pradyumna Karan *The Non-Western World: Environment, Development and Human Rights*. New York: Routledge, 2004.

Paul M. Kennedy *The Parliament of Man: The Past, Present, and Future of the United Nations*. New York: Random House, 2006.

Sanford Levinson *Torture: A Collection*. New York: Oxford University Press, 2004.

George Lodge *A Corporate Solution to Global Poverty: How Multinationals Can Help and Craig Wilson the Poor and Invigorate Their Own Legitimacy*. Princeton, NJ: Princeton University Press, 2007.

Michael J. Matheson — *Council Unbound: The Growth of UN Decision Making on Conflict and Post-conflict Issues after the Cold War.* Washington, DC: USIP, 2006.

Mark McGillivray and Matthew Clarke — *Understanding Human Well-being.* Tokyo, Japan: United Nations University (UNU) Press, 2006.

Julie Mertus and Jeffrey Helsing — *Human Rights and Conflict: Exploring the Links Between Rights, Law, and Peacebuilding.* Washington, DC: USIP, 2006.

Mahmood Monshipouri, Neil Englehart, Andrew J. Nathan, and Kavita Philip — *Constructing Human Rights in the Age of Globalization* Armonk, NY: M.E. Sharpe, 2003.

Jonathan D. Moreno — *In the Wake of Terror: Medicine and Morality in a Time of Crisis.* Cambridge, MA: MIT Press, 2003.

Ronald Niezen — *The Origins of Indigenism: Human Rights and the Politics of Identity.* Berkeley: University of California Press, 2003.

John O'Manique — *The Origins of Justice: The Evolution of Morality, Human Rights and Law.* Philadelphia: University of Pennsylvania Press, 2003

Brian Orend — *Human Rights: Concept and Context.* Peterborough, ON: Broadview, 2001.

Thomas Pogge — *World Poverty and Human Rights.* Cambridge: Polity, 2002.

Eric Reeves

A Long Day's Dying: Critical Moments in the Darfur Genocide. Toronto: Key, 2007.

Kenneth Roth, Minky Worden, and Amy D. Bernstein

Torture: Does it Make Us Safer? Is it Ever Ok? New York: The New Press, 2005.

John H.F. Shattuck

Freedom on Fire: Human Rights Wars and America's Response. Cambridge, MA: Harvard University Press, 2003.

William F. Schulz

Tainted Legacy: 9/11 and the Ruin of Human Rights. New York: Thunder's Mouth Press/Nation Books, 2003.

Thomas D. Williams

Who is My Neighbor? Personalism and the Foundations of Human Rights. Washington, DC: The Catholic University of America (CUA) Press, 2005.

John Yoo

War By Other Means. New York: Atlantic Monthly, 2006.

Index